LEADING A
LEGACY

Leading a Legacy

How Leaders Build Resilient Teams and Create Lasting Impact

William E. Mojica

Published by Game Changer Publishing

Paperback ISBN: 979-8-90158-093-6

Hardcover ISBN: 979-8-90158-094-3

Digital ISBN: 979-8-90158-095-0

|GC| GAME CHANGER
PUBLISHING

www.GameChangerPublishing.com

DEDICATION

William

William, our firstborn—you began it all. From the moment you entered this world, I saw my life take shape through your eyes. Now, standing taller than me, you carry not just height but a presence filled with wisdom, humility, and heart.

Your brilliance shines in how you think, learn, and love. You challenge the status quo with grace, and your faith is not just spoken—it's lived. You make people feel seen, valued, and cared for, leading not with noise but with quiet strength and compassion.

You are a leader in every sense—someone who lifts others, takes responsibility, and moves forward with purpose. Watching you grow into the man you are today fills me with pride and awe. You are everything I hoped for and more.

William, you are a blessing. Your legacy is already unfolding in the lives you touch. The world is better because of your love, your faith, and your heart. I couldn't be prouder to call you my son.

Henry

Henry, my son, you've taught me more about passion than anyone I've ever known. From your earliest steps, I saw a fire in you—a drive to compete, grow, and rise above expectations. Your strength is undeniable, but it's your heart that humbles me most.

You care deeply for others, making people feel seen, heard, and valued. You lead with kindness, empathy, and quiet wisdom far beyond your years. You're not just strong; you're courageous. A leader who stands firm in faith and conviction, even when the path is hard.

Our early mornings together, reading Scripture and talking about life, are moments I'll always treasure. Your love for God and your desire to follow His path fills me with peace and pride.

Henry, you are a remarkable young man. I couldn't be prouder of the way you live, lead, and love. Your journey will be one of purpose, and I'll be cheering you on every step of the way.

Oliver

Oliver, you are a remarkable soul—sharp, witty, and full of wonder. From the start, you've seen the world differently, finding humor and beauty in places others overlook. You light up every room with your laughter and insight, turning ordinary moments into something unforgettable.

Your curiosity runs deep. You ask the hard questions, challenge assumptions, and never settle for surface answers. You see beyond what's obvious, and your hunger for truth makes you wise beyond your years. You lead with thoughtfulness and courage, inspiring others to think, laugh, and grow.

Your love for Jesus moves me most. The way you seek Him with sincerity and depth is a gift. Our conversations about faith are treasures I'll carry forever. You're not just learning; you're leading with conviction and heart.

And Oliver, what I admire most is your fearless spirit. You don't shy away from complexity—you lean into it. You're a courageous thinker and a bold leader, unafraid to question, explore, and stand firm in what you believe. That strength, paired with your compassion, will shape lives and lead a legacy of light.

I'm so proud of the young man you're becoming. Keep questioning, keep laughing, and keep shining your light. You are a true gift to our family and to the world.

Winston

Winston, you are a reflection of the passion and curiosity I had at your age. From the moment you could walk and talk, your love for all things mechanical was clear. Whether we're talking shop or tinkering with cars, I'm constantly amazed by your mind—always learning, always exploring, always improving.

You see life as a puzzle, and you're always searching for the next piece to make it better. Your instinct for innovation and drive for excellence is rare and powerful. You don't settle for "good enough"—you aim to make things great, and that mindset will carry you far.

But what moves me most is your heart. You seek truth with sincerity, asking big questions about life and faith, always wanting to understand what matters most. Your love for God runs deep, and your journey of faith is one I'm honored to witness.

You fiercely protect those you love, especially your brothers, with loyalty and pride. You carry our family's values with strength and grace, and your words and actions reflect a heart full of love.

Winston, you are a young man of extraordinary character. Your mechanical mind, your hunger to grow, your devotion to God, and your love for family will shape a legacy that lasts. I'm so proud of you—keep building, keep seeking, and keep leading with the heart of a protector and a faithful son.

To My Bride

Hilary, my love—my partner and the heart of our home. From the very beginning, you've walked beside me with grace and strength, through seasons of uncertainty, sacrifice, and growth. When comfort was scarce and the future unclear, you never wavered. You believed in the vision, in us, and in the purpose that carried us forward. You gave me the freedom to dream and the courage to pursue it.

You've been my anchor—steady when the winds blew hardest. When I lost my footing, you reminded me who I was. You lifted me when I was weary, challenged me when I needed truth, and stood beside me with unwavering love. You've helped me see the beauty in every person, every moment, and every chapter of this journey we've written together.

Together, we've raised four incredible boys, each a reflection of your wisdom, compassion, and faith. You didn't just join my vision; you shaped it, strengthened it, and made it ours. The legacy we're building is as much yours as mine, and I am endlessly grateful for the way you've poured your heart into every step.

Your love for Christ is the foundation of our family. I've watched you live your faith with quiet strength and radiant grace. You seek truth with humility, and you love with a depth that inspires everyone around you. You've created a home where kindness thrives, where our boys are nurtured, and where God's presence is felt in every corner.

Hilary, you are the soul of this journey. Your love is timeless, your faith unshakable, and your heart a reflection of everything good and true. I couldn't have asked for a better partner in life. Thank you for being the one who makes it all possible. You are my greatest blessing, and I will love you forever.

ADVANCE PRAISE

"*Leading a Legacy* is a practical guide for leaders who want to build strong teams and a culture that performs when it counts. It comes from a leader who actually gets it and who is an all-too-rare combination of technical and soft skills, experience, and a laser focus on building a learning and speak-up culture. William wisely focuses on identifying and reducing risk to his company while also respecting and developing its teammates. As he has taught me, feedback is a blessing. If one is deaf to it, they may also be blind to any wisdom it may contain."

— **Jeffrey D. Wiese, Former Associate Administrator for Pipeline Safety, U.S. DOT/PHMSA; Former Senior Vice President, TRC Companies (Pipeline Integrity Services)**

"*Leading a Legacy* is an important reminder that real leadership is measured by the culture you build and the standards you refuse to compromise—especially when safety and public trust are at stake. William Mojica sets an example for both current and aspiring leaders to follow as they work to make the world a better place. In this book, he offers practical, values-driven guidance for leaders responsible for people, communities, and critical infrastructure. I have seen William in action, personifying everything he covers in this book, making this a clear and credible call to lead with accountability and leave an enduring legacy."

— Alan K. Mayberry, Former Associate Administrator for Pipeline Safety, U.S. DOT/PHMSA

"This book addresses the tension leaders live in between preparation and trust—knowing challenges will come while believing God remains in control. It confronts the tendency to drift toward either passivity or self-reliance and instead calls leaders to honor God through intentional planning and wholehearted surrender. Through stories from William's career and childhood, the book highlights diligence, discipline, culture, and commitment as essential practices in the daily battle of capable leadership that learns to trust God."

— Mark Artrip, Lead Pastor, Movement Church in Hilliard, Ohio

"I've worked closely with William Mojica and have witnessed firsthand the commitment, integrity, discipline, and care he brings to leadership. *Leading a Legacy* is a leadership tutorial for business that reflects those same qualities, offering practical insights for leaders who wish to build resilient teams and strengthen organizations through their leadership. Very thoughtful and evocative!"

— Dwight D. Keen, Commissioner, Kansas Corporation Commission

"Every manager—whether an emerging leader or a seasoned veteran—should read this book. William brings leadership to life through real stories and practical examples that show what strong, values-based leadership looks like in any situation.

Having had the privilege of working closely with him for several years, I've seen firsthand that this book reflects how he truly leads. William remains grounded in his core values and consistently walks his talk, day in and day out. He leads his legacy every day—demonstrating that when people and safety are placed at the center of leadership, everything else follows."

— Elizabeth M. Ruske, Managing Partner and CEO of Tiara Leadership LLC

"I've watched William invest in people, not just outcomes, and that's why his leadership endures—true leaders don't measure success by how well they perform, but by how many new leaders they help rise."

— **Patrick Vieth**

"William Mojica is one of the most earnest Americans I know. William's wisdom and perspective on how to increase American energy, American lives, and our freedoms is to be followed and enjoyed for all those willing to share his boldness and purpose."

— **Tricia Pridemore, Georgia Public Service Commisioner**

READ THIS FIRST

Thanks for buying and reading my book.
I would like to connect!

Scan the QR code here:

LEADING A LEGACY

How Leaders Build
Resilient Teams and
Create *Lasting Impact*

WILLIAM E. MOJICA

FOREWORD

In *Leading a Legacy*, Mojica has written THE leadership bible that leaders and future leaders should rush to read. I have seen Mojica sit at the table responding to more than one black swan event where everyone in the room, from the lowest-level employee to the CEO, has followed his wise counsel as he led them through the aftermath. His storytelling is poignant, his counsel transcends the mere dollars and cents, and it enters the realm of the spiritual. He teaches us that prioritizing people and safety, building trust through service, and maintaining a reputation above reproach creates a "light-house effect." By projecting a clear vision that inspires others to uphold and improve it, one builds a truly profound legacy. For Mojica, leading a legacy is not only for business but also for his life and that of his four sons. Leaders would be wise to follow his prophecy.

– **Cynthia L. Quarterman** is a lawyer and engineer who served as Administrator of PHMSA at the U.S. Department of Transportation. Before that, she was Director of the U.S. Department of the Interior's Minerals Management Service. She holds a degree in industrial engineering from Northwestern University and a Juris Doctor from Columbia Law School.

CONTENTS

INTRODUCTION

"…From everyone who has been given much, much will be demanded; and from the one who has been entrusted with much, much more will be asked."
Luke 12:48 NIV

Legacy has captivated me for as long as I can remember. My interest in legacy began at an early age as I listened to stories told by relatives and friends around the dinner table. Their experiences left a powerful imprint on our family. Growing up in Panama, I heard many stories of individuals who worked hard, their lives becoming the stuff of local legend. These stories were shared at sports outings, in restaurants, and even during public speeches meant to honor those who had come before us. Hearing these stories encouraged me to make a positive impact in my own life.

The story that comes to mind most vividly is about my grandmother, Melida Mojica, a name I carry with pride. What resonates most deeply with me when we talk about legacy is the incredible and lasting impact she left on the city of Santiago, Panama.

Every single day, she led that legacy.

In her small community, she accomplished so much. She brought people together to build schools and basketball courts and developed programs that taught underprivileged mothers how to bake and cook so they could provide for their families. Growing up, I remember visiting her during the summers, and her house was always filled with people. It was common for someone to walk in without knocking, asking for her help. They would sit at the dinner table with her, sharing their needs and struggles. Some had walked for hours seeking a little money for medicine or help finding work.

There was a man who stopped by her house regularly. He would collect the best *estropajos* (loofahs, in English), clean them up, and sell them to my grandmother; this was one of the many jobs he would do for my grandparents. She always found ways to help those in need. If someone came asking for money to feed their family, she would find them yard work to do. And at times, she also used her community and political influence to help those who had no other path forward.

She is still known for stepping into situations others avoided. On one occasion, local Panamanian police were brutally beating a drunk man in the street. While blows were still falling, my grandmother moved into the middle of it, placing her body between batons and flesh, forcing the violence to stop. In that moment, the man was her community—he was her son, and he was everything she stood for: people.

Her legacy was about the people of Santiago, Panama: caring for them, challenging them, equipping them, and helping those with the greatest need find a way out of their circumstances. Her legacy has stood the test of time, and it continues to live on.

She set an example for me, demonstrating how to lead a legacy through everyday actions. Years have passed since my grandmother died, but when I return to Santiago, Panama, most people may not recognize me. Some might know my parents, but when I tell them I am the grandson of Melida and Meliton (my grandfather) Mojica, there is immediate recognition. Her powerful imprint on that town remains.

I believe that's what leading a legacy is all about. We all have the opportunity to make a difference wherever we are. My grandmother chose to be an educator in the country of Panama, but her actions extended far beyond her profession. Her actions carried into her community and left a mark that continues to echo through time.

As I moved through school, I learned about pioneers who shaped American and world history, as well as local heroes, relatives, family friends, and others who left lasting legacies. Learning the stories of those who came before me helped me appreciate that most individuals long to understand their purpose in life. Many leaders embark on their leadership journey with a desire to leave a lasting impact—a legacy that will endure beyond their years.

Throughout my career, I have learned from incredible leaders whose wisdom I have passed on to those I have served. I have been blessed by strong men and women who invested in me, allowing me to grow in my own leadership journey.

My parents are among those leaders. They demonstrated a deep passion for people of all walks of life and intentionally blessed my sisters and me with a broad perspective on culture and society. They valued people more than anything else. Their dedication to giving their time and support to others is an example that will take me a lifetime to model. They spent endless hours helping those in need while continuing to support our family.

In 2023, *Rolling Stone* magazine published an article titled "Legacy of Leadership: 5 Profound Lessons My Grandfather Taught Me for Business Success."[1] The piece offers one man's reflection on legacy and the importance of thinking about it early in life. The author describes his grandfather's legacy not in terms of accomplishments, but in values, generosity, and how he treated people. He said, "My grandfather's legacy is his values, his generosity, and the way he treated people and made them feel valuable. That's the kind of legacy I want. At some point, everyone has to face the thought of what they'll leave behind, but as a leader, you'll leave part of your legacy with every person you lead. So, how are you making a positive impact on those people's lives? How will they remember you?"

1. Hennessey, J. (2023, December 7). Legacy of Leadership: 5 profound lessons My grandfather taught me for business success. *Rolling Stone.* https://www.rollingstone.com/culture-council/articles/legacy-leadership-5-profound-lessons-grandfather-taught-me-business-success-1234917905/

We have all been shaped by the legacies of those who have come before us. And now, we each have the opportunity to lead a legacy of our own—in our families, friendships, communities, and organizations. Our actions today ripple outward, shaping how we will be remembered and, more importantly, how others will live and lead because of us.

This book is dedicated to transforming a concept we often hear about into something lived and meaningful. While many people focus on *leaving* a legacy, I challenge you to embrace the idea of *leading* one, quietly shifting from "V" to "D." This shift—from passive reflection to daily responsibility— changes how we show up as leaders. It changes how we make decisions. It places people and safety at the center of leadership, not as a theory, but as a lived commitment.

Leadership is both a privilege and a calling. It is an honor entrusted to us by God, and one that carries profound responsibility. This book invites you to reflect on that responsibility—not someday, but today.

Many of us in the workforce spend more time with peers and employees than with our own families. It may not be something we should necessarily promote, but it often takes up the best part of our day, and we must consider how we spend our energy and effort with those we lead. No matter our industry or profession, we share our time, life stories, aspirations, struggles, and successes with each other. We don't just work together; we go through life together, through the good and the bad, making our workplaces ripe opportunities to lead a legacy.

My goal is for you to view this as a legacy playbook filled with key items that can't be missed throughout your leadership journey. You will discover essential principles that must be prioritized to be successful. Each day, we have a choice to take intentional steps in how we lead our people, and the lessons in this book will help you do just that.

WHY LEGACY?

When asked, one might be quick to associate profits with success and a positive legacy, but I'm here to turn this thinking on its head. While profit is important to business, it's not the most important. The message in society is that financial success means you made it, but this could not be further from the truth. The moment one walks into a publicly traded company, it is made abundantly clear that the ticker price for the stock is one of the most important indicators of the business's success. Yet, how many times have we seen companies fail to deliver on the foundational needs of the business, resulting in high profits and an unhealthy company culture? What if there were another metric that was more important than profits?

It is important to pause here and set the record straight. Solid financial performance is essential for any company that aims to continuously invest back in its sustainability, whether by investing in its people, assets, or any of the company's core strategies. But *starting* with profits will never allow us to achieve the appropriate results.

Rather than starting with a vision for profits, I argue for starting with a vision for legacy.

To lead a legacy, we must prioritize people and safety over profits, foster a strong company culture, and learn from past tragedies to prevent future failures. Over the next eleven chapters, we will focus on the significance of legacy in leadership, stemming from firsthand experiences and historical lessons within corporate environments. We will reflect on the importance of mentoring, preparing emerging leaders, and consistently recalling foundational lessons, all while building long-lasting cultures where people come first. You will walk away with the tools to embed intentional values in your company that ensure a positive, lasting impact on your team and community.

Remember: *You don't live your life to <u>leave</u> a legacy…you live your life to <u>lead</u> a legacy.*

HOW TO USE THIS BOOK

As I wrote this book, I kept coming back to one central truth: leading a legacy is not something you turn on and off. It isn't a title, a role, or a position. It's who you are at work, at home, in private, and in public. It's how you show up in every space you enter and how you leave people, teams, and communities better because you were there.

That's why I've intentionally shared stories from both my personal and professional life. Leadership is not compartmentalized. It's integrated. Your character, values, habits, faith, and decisions don't stay in separate lanes; they shape how you lead, how you serve, and how you influence others every day.

My hope is that as you read this book, you will pause often. Reflect deeply. Ask yourself not only how you *want* to show up as a leader, but also how you are actually showing up today. The growth happens in that gap, and growth, when pursued honestly and intentionally, becomes transformation.

In chapter 10, I share practical tools to help you continue developing, not just as a leader, but as someone committed to leading a legacy that outlives any role, title, or season.

At the end of each chapter, you'll find a **Get to Work** section. These aren't reflections for reflection's sake; they are designed to move you into action immediately. Don't skip them. Leadership is built through application, not accumulation. Read slowly. Think deeply. Do the work.

This book isn't meant to be consumed. It's meant to be lived.

1

PREPARING THE HORSE FOR BATTLE

"The horse is made ready for the day of battle,
but victory rests with the Lord."
Proverbs 21:31 NIV

I began my career at Exxon as an engineering intern in New Orleans, Louisiana, in the summer of 1999. My understanding of corporate America was limited, and I didn't know what to expect when I arrived at Exxon. Even though I was inexperienced, I was motivated and refused to let anything get in the way of my learning and development.

I worked for Southwest Gas Corporation out of their Tucson, Arizona, office during the school year, supporting their franchise or public improvement department. I spent my summers traveling through the Louisiana, Florida, and Texas territories within the Exxon footprint, learning where petroleum came from and how it was extracted from the ground, processed, and transported around the world. I learned about petroleum and natural gas reserves and the impact of petrochemicals, including hydrocarbons, diesels, gasoline, propane, and methane (natural gas), on our lives.

I had the opportunity to take on a variety of assignments, from reservoir engineering to pipeline design, and one of my favorites was subsea pipeline engineering. I arrived at the company with a badge that read Exxon, and less than a month later, the company badge would never read the same again, as Exxon finalized the merger with Mobil, forming one of the largest oil companies in the world, ExxonMobil. Their footprint would expand worldwide, and later in my career, it would give me the opportunity to work on pipeline projects that stretched from Indonesia to Sakhalin Island to New York. Exxon was a great place for me to begin my career. The leadership and staff were hospitable and took pride in welcoming every new intern. It was a wonderful opportunity for me to experience the importance of working as a team. At Exxon, I also learned one of the most valuable components of my leadership: a passion for people and safety.

Later, I came to realize that the culture of safety that roamed the halls of Exxon was indicative of a company that had learned from the past. The Exxon Valdez spill of 1989 was a lasting example of what happens when companies fail to deliver on their commitments and don't place people and safety at the heart of everything they do.

It is rare for me to mention the Exxon Valdez in a public setting without people knowing what I'm talking about.

However, looking back at one of the most tragic incidents in Exxon's history, it's crucial to understand what happened.

The Exxon Valdez was a tanker that struck a reef in Prince William Sound, Alaska. The ship veered out of its normal shipping lanes and collided with the reef, resulting in the release of approximately eleven million gallons of crude oil into the water.

The environmental damage was massive. The spill contaminated hundreds of miles of coastline and killed significant numbers of birds, fish, and marine mammals, devastating local communities and fisheries for years to come. In reviewing what happened, it becomes clear that fatigue played a critical role. The officer navigating the ship had not gotten enough sleep and was likely exhausted when the tanker hit the reef. Moreover, there were not enough crew members on board. Exxon had reduced crew size to cut costs, placing excessive responsibility on the remaining employees. Overtime was encouraged and praised in performance reviews, while adequate rest was not prioritized. Employees were evaluated on the amount of extra work they did, which pressured them to remain on duty even when tired.

There was no effective system in place to track work hours. Although rules regarding work and rest hours existed on paper, the company did not adequately enforce adherence to these guidelines. Furthermore, there were no guarantees of having a rested backup officer on duty. When the ship departed from port, there was no requirement for another well-rested officer to assist on the bridge.

The risks associated with fatigue were ignored. The National Transportation Safety Board stated that Exxon did not demonstrate sufficient concern for the dangers posed by long hours and tired crews. This was not merely a case of one negligent captain; investigators identified these problems as indicative of a broader, weak safety culture within the company.

By the time I started at Exxon a decade later, they had learned from their mistakes. A sense of learning permeated the company culture, and they were more prepared to handle demanding situations as they arose. Exxon had developed processes and procedures that enabled more consistent approaches to our work, while also investing in state-of-the-art training that modeled a college classroom setting, with dedicated instructors who invested in our learning and development throughout our careers.

From day one on the job, it was clear that our development and preparation were key; Exxon was equipping us to tackle tough industry problems in a safe and effective manner. We grew from these learnings, allowing us to pass them on to the companies we would ultimately lead beyond our time there. Through these learnings, we have continued to raise the industry bench by not forgetting what can happen when companies reprioritize what matters and sacrifice the essential building blocks of their culture.

While the Exxon Valdez spill might seem unique, through my career, I've encountered similar issues in various settings. No matter the industry, incidents can occur when we fail to prioritize safety.

CREATING COMPANY CULTURE EVERY DAY

In many ways, the work we do and how we do it is a gift we leave behind for those who are coming after us. We can choose whether the gift is good or bad. It's our decision to lead a positive legacy or a negative one for those who will follow us. I'm sure we've all experienced the opposite, when we are left with a mess to clean up. In this situation, we must rebuild an already fragile company culture one brick at a time. Throughout my career, I've encouraged people to see beyond the immediate results of their labor. When we lead, we work to ensure the next generation of leaders has a solid foundation to build on. And through our actions, we begin to weave the fabric of company culture. This doesn't happen overnight; it stretches over time to make a lasting impact on the communities we serve.

I tell my employees that we need to make it difficult for future leaders to change the positive and meaningful impact we are making by creating a culture where people cannot live any other way. This leads our people to continue to press leadership on what good looks like and challenges leadership to be better every day. Once people have seen the promised land, there's no turning back. That's how we maintain momentum. That's how we maintain a positive culture that can't be easily broken over time.

As I look back on my time at Exxon, I think about the new generation of leaders we are creating today. Are we preparing them to face the challenges ahead? Are we giving them the tools to prioritize people and safety? Are we challenging them on their purpose and the gifts they will leave behind? Are we preparing the horse for battle by establishing foundations within our culture that will not be broken down over time?

At the start of my career at Exxon, one of my mentors, Natalie, provided me with the opportunity to explore the project I was assigned to, which involved working on a pipeline system to make it more efficient and increase production. One impactful experience she facilitated was a trip to New London, Texas, where a tragic school explosion occurred on March 18, 1937. As we traveled through small towns to get there, passing by hills, farmlands, rivers, lakes, local grocery stores, and gas stations, she began to explain why our jobs were so important and why we needed to understand the risks of transporting a highly flammable product. She shared that when things don't go right in our industry, the results can significantly impact the people we serve.

When we arrived at the memorial, the weight of the place settled on me immediately. It was quiet in a way that felt heavy, almost reverent, as if the ground itself remembered what had happened there. Standing still, I found myself imagining that day not as a single moment, but as hundreds of lives interrupted at once. Children of every age, from the smallest, who were just beginning to understand the world, to high school students already forming dreams of who they might become. In an instant, all of it was gone.

My mind drifted to what that day must have felt like inside the school, the confusion, the fear, the force of the explosion tearing through classrooms and hallways. And then my thoughts moved beyond the building to the parents and the community. I imagined them running toward the rubble, pushing through smoke and debris, calling out names, searching desperately for any sign of life. The waiting. The silence. The unbearable realization that many would never hear their child's voice again. As those images formed, I felt a deep drop in my heart—an ache so heavy it was almost physical.

At the time, I couldn't have known what that feeling meant. I had no way of understanding that it would return or that it would one day surface in the middle of my own career. Standing there, I only knew that something had lodged itself deep within me—a quiet awareness that tragedy leaves more than destruction behind. It leaves responsibility.

Years later, that same feeling would rise again. I would travel to California to help support a community after a tragic pipeline explosion. This time, I would not be alone. I would be there with my wife—the wife I didn't have yet—and alongside children who had not yet been born when I first stood at that memorial. Later, as we drove through the affected San Bruno neighborhood, the heaviness returned in full. Different place. Different moment. The same unmistakable weight in my chest.

Only then did I fully understand that what I experienced at a young age was not fleeting. It was formative. It had been quietly shaping how I viewed safety, leadership, and accountability long before I realized those views would define my work. That early encounter with loss and consequence had been a foreshadowing, one that would later guide me when tragedy was no longer something I was learning about but something I was called to respond to.

The 1937 explosion itself was the result of an unscented natural gas leak that had been migrating throughout the school for weeks. When a shop class began using an electric sander, the spark ignited the gas, causing an explosion that killed more than 290 people, including children and school staff. That single event permanently changed the natural gas industry. Today, the natural gas delivered to our homes and businesses is intentionally scented with mercaptan, a distinctive rotten-egg odor, so leaks can be detected before disaster strikes. It is a safety measure born from unimaginable loss, quietly protecting communities every day.

Looking back, I realize that standing at that memorial did more than teach me history. It awakened something in me—a lasting understanding that behind every system, every regulation, and every technical decision are real people and real lives. That realization took hold early, and it would go on to shape not just the leader I became but also the responsibility I carry.

Although Natalie had only been out of college for a handful of years, she was remarkable in her role. That summer at Exxon, she took me under her wing and did so much to train and develop me. I felt comfortable asking her any questions, no matter how trivial, but I would not have felt comfortable doing so in a larger group at the time.

But what impressed me most was her care and wisdom at such a young age. Despite our close ages, she was able to connect with me on a level that left a lasting impression. I doubt she realizes the impact she had on me, but her leadership and commitment to safety created a legacy that I carry with me. I am truly thankful for her guidance, which has influenced my entire career.

During our visit, Natalie made it clear to me that safety had to be at the core of my career and that I needed to learn from this event so I could play a role in ensuring events like this would never happen again. What I didn't know then is that her wisdom would serve as a foundation for how I would lead my teams when the time came.

I share this story and the incident with my teams every March, reminding them of the legacy that Natalie has left behind and the impact we can have on our employees. The London School is a reminder that we must be continually learning so that we can prevent incidents like this from happening.

Later in my career, I was present in Houston, Texas, when the company said goodbye to Lee Raymond as CEO of ExxonMobil. In a large auditorium in downtown Houston, Raymond was asked about the proudest moment in his career, as well as the most challenging.

He responded that he was most proud of the merger between Exxon and Mobil. Raymond also shared that he would always remember the tragedy of Valdez.

As I heard Raymond speak that day, I realized that to rise through a company and leave a lasting and positive legacy, I would have to be prepared to face challenges along with successes. I began to understand that my career would not be defined by my accomplishments alone, but by how I handled the opportunities placed before me to shape culture and invest in people. I realized that preparation for challenges would be important, so I became grounded in learning how to keep companies out of trouble by operating safely while also leading companies through tough challenges. I began focusing not only on setting the tone for the company's culture but also on ensuring that employees are well prepared for anything that may come.

Even after I left ExxonMobil, the company's culture of people and safety stayed with me. I carried it into every organization that followed, often without realizing it. The lessons I learned there prepared me for some of the most difficult moments of my career, including two of the most tragic natural gas pipeline events in U.S. history: the September 2010 Natural Gas Transmission Pipeline Rupture and Fire in San Bruno, California, and the September 2018 Merrimack Valley Overpressurization of Natural Gas Distribution System, Explosions, and Fires in Massachusetts.

When I arrived in California, it became clear that I would need to testify before the California Public Utilities Commission about the programs we were proposing to improve system integrity and strengthen the safety of our gas network.

As I prepared for that moment, I felt a weight gathering across my shoulders, heavy, insistent, and almost physical. I knew the judge or interveners might look at me and ask, "Mr. Mojica, have you visited the site? Do you understand the severity of what happened here, after eight people lost their lives?"

I couldn't walk into that room without being able to answer those questions honestly. I couldn't risk someone mistaking my lack of a site visit for a lack of care. More importantly, I couldn't live with myself if I didn't fully understand the human cost of what happened.

So I chose an evening to visit the site. At that time, Hilary and I had two boys, and after dinner we drove together to the neighborhood. The closer we got, the quieter we both became. The air inside the car felt dense, like the gravity of the place was pressing inward. Neither of us needed to speak; we could both feel the weight of where we were headed.

When we turned onto the street where the incident had occurred, a tightness formed in my chest. The neighborhood looked split in two. Rebuilt homes stood clean and sharp, their exteriors almost too bright under the streetlights. Just beyond them, the older homes sat in somber contrast— weathered, familiar, and untouched by the reconstruction. That contrast lingered in my mind long after we passed it.

As we drove slowly, I imagined families inside those homes on the evening of the explosion: kids finishing homework, parents cooking dinner, people settling into the comfort of a normal evening. Those small, everyday images are inter- twined with the reality that eight people never made it out. The thought left a lump in my throat.

I looked toward the rebuilt section and tried to imagine the flames, the panic, and the loss. The wind carried the faint smells of the San Francisco Bay, while my imagination infused the smell of burning throughout the neighborhood. Hilary stood quietly beside me, taking in the same scene. Even without words, I could sense she felt the weight of it too, the shared understanding that this was more than a tragic event; it was a reminder of the responsibility carried by those who work in our industry.

The responsibility pressed against me more heavily than any job title ever had. We transport a flammable product under pressure beneath the streets where people live their entire lives; moments like this made that truth impossible to ignore. I remembered what Natalie had told me so many years before when we visited the New London School.

That evening changed something in me.

My leadership years during that period became what I now call "compressed years"—six years that aged me fifteen. The gravity of these risks affected how I slept, how intensely I reviewed decisions, and how little tolerance I had for short-cuts or superficial fixes. At home, I was more present in some ways and distant in others, torn between being a father and being responsible for preventing the next tragedy. The stakes were too high for anything less than full commitment.

Looking back, that visit to San Bruno was a turning point. The contrast of the homes, the stillness of the neighborhood, and the quiet unity between Hilary and me that evening shaped a deeper sense of duty within me. It wasn't just about regulatory compliance or technical upgrades; it was about honoring the lives affected and committing to ensuring that such a tragedy never happens again.

These experiences have given me a unique perspective. I have seen how tragedies ripple through communities, through employees, and through a company's reputation. And from them, I have learned the importance of preparation and the need to build organizations firmly grounded in what truly matters: protecting people, anticipating risks, and never forgetting the human beings behind every decision.

I would encourage everyone to reflect on the threats present in their own industries and consider how those threats could materialize in ways that might harm others. For me, San Bruno was beyond a case study; it was a profound reminder that leadership is not only about guiding teams or delivering results. It is about carrying the weight of responsibility for the lives that depend on our decisions and doing everything in our power to ensure that history does not repeat itself.

No matter the industry we are in, events can happen, and challenges will arise. And if we want to lead a legacy, it all starts with preparation. Have we created a culture that's equipped to prevent significant events, handle them if they occur, and prevent them from happening again? Are our teams prepared for whatever may come?

Proverbs 21:31 (NLT) says, *"The horse is prepared for the day of battle, but the victory belongs to the Lord."* In summary, preparing the horse for battle does not guarantee victory, but it allows the soldier to know that they have done everything possible to get the horse ready for what lies ahead. In biblical times, a warhorse was crucial for safety. It still needed to be fed, trained, and outfitted with armor to be ready for battle. This illustrates the importance of doing everything humanly possible to be prepared and responsible.

Faith is not an excuse for laziness. In fact, the verse counters the notion that God will handle everything, so we don't need to prepare. It says the opposite: you should prepare thoroughly and trust God with the outcomes. Good preparation honors God and protects people. Preparing the horse signifies that you care about the soldiers' lives and their mission.

Today, this principle applies to safety culture, planning, training, and risk management. While you don't control everything, you are accountable for how seriously you prepare. Why is this preparation important? Horses were the tanks of their time. A trained horse could turn the tide of a battle by providing speed and power. Conversely, a poorly prepared horse could endanger all. If a horse panicked, slipped, or became exhausted too quickly, it could jeopardize the soldier, the unit, and even the entire battle line. Preparation demonstrates a commitment to protecting lives.

Kings and commanders who took the time to prepare their horses, chariots, and gear demonstrated that they valued their soldiers, rather than merely hoping that God would fix anything that went wrong.

So how did they prepare for battle? They fed and conditioned the horses. Horses received food, water, and regular exercise to build strength and endurance for long marches. They were trained to recognize loud sounds without becoming spooked.

Warhorses were exposed to chaos and fear, including loud noises, drums, crowds, and weapons, to prevent them from bolting when battle became loud and fierce. This training focused on obedience and control, teaching the horses to respond quickly to reins, leg, and voice cues, even when frightened. Equipment and protection were essential, too. Depending on the era and region, horses might be fitted with saddles, special harnesses for chariots, and sometimes light armor to shield their bodies. Conducting readiness checks for battle was crucial. Just like we inspect our gear today, soldiers and handlers would check the horses' hooves, legs, tack, reins, and overall condition before heading into battle.

In the end, while the horse is prepared for battle, the victory belongs to the Lord. This emphasizes a fundamental truth: you put in the hard, detailed work of preparation, right down to checking the horses' hooves and harness, and then recognize that the ultimate outcomes are in God's hands.

As leaders, we must control what we can and avoid getting trapped in what we cannot. It is our role as leaders to prepare our people for battle and to guide them through not only the successful parts of our daily operations but also the rough patches. We must prepare the horse for battle.

I remember being asked to help a company through a rough patch after an event, and during our first formal meeting, the CEO made a powerful observation that he shared with me. He said, "William, last year, when we were closing out the year and discussing our year-end safety performance, the team relayed that it was our best safety year ever. When I asked them how we got here, they couldn't explain it; they couldn't break down for me the steps they had taken to win the year. I didn't prod any further, but I should have; the incident happened shortly after." That conversation has been embedded in my brain as a reminder that the absence of incidents in a company's culture isn't an indication of a healthy safety culture. Today, more than ever, I understand what Todd Conklin's commonly used statement truly means with respect to safety: "Safety is not the absence of events; safety is the presence of defenses." Not experiencing safety events, or having what are perceived to be good safety numbers at the end of the year without being able to explain how we got there or understand if we have the appropriate metrics does not indicate an appropriate safety culture at work.

For many years, people often cited declining incident rates as proof that safety was improving. On the surface, the data appeared to support that belief. However, a closer look revealed a critical flaw. The incidents that were decreasing were not always the ones that carried the greatest risk.

As an industry, we became very effective at tracking and reducing lower-risk events such as slips, trips, falls, and minor injuries, while giving far less attention to high-consequence incidents. The outcome was predictable. Minor incidents declined, but serious and fatal events remained largely unchanged. When these were combined into a single metric, it created the appearance of progress. In reality, the events most likely to cost a life were not improving at all.

This is why the absence of incidents does not equal the presence of safety. Low incident rates alone do not reflect a strong safety culture. Without understanding which incidents are declining, why they are declining, and whether the right indicators are being measured, organizations risk mistaking fewer accidents for genuine safety.

As I've studied and interacted with great and timeless leaders, I've discovered something they have in common: an unquenchable yet balanced approach to winning. They are passionate about people and safety, and they have a constant vision of leading a legacy. A mature leader understands that risk cannot be completely removed and that we often cannot guarantee how our efforts will be received by external stakeholders, the media, or our own employees. These leaders understand that by responding appropriately, we can enhance the outcomes of our vision, passion, and legacy.

THE MYTH OF ZERO RISK

How many leaders have you met who are risk-averse? How often have you heard the phrase "Zero incidents is achievable" roaming the halls of your company?

When we talk about zero incidents, we don't always understand what that means. Time and time again, I have watched my team achieve zero serious incidents, incidents that keep them from going home to their families in the same way that they came to work. While that is great, there is a better question to ask: "What incidents are we talking about and trying to prevent?"

Todd Conklin says it best in his book *Workplace Fatalities: Failure to Predict*: [1]

---

1. Conklin, T. (2017). *Workplace Fatalities: Failure to Predict* (1st ed.). CreateSpace Independent Publishing Platform.

Zero is killing people. This is the most interesting artifact of the old safety thinking. Zero seems like such a perfect goal for safety. Zero accidents, zero harm, zero injuries, zero events, all of these ideas sound so good and so attractive. All of these zeros are simply not possible and will never be possible. Your organization places its entire future in the hands of smart, yet unreliable human operators. You will not get to zero. You will never sustain zero. Asking for zero actually reduces your operational knowledge. If you want zero events, I can almost guarantee greatly reduced reporting of events of all sizes and shapes. You've heard it. You have said it. Zero accidents are attainable. This idea is just so wrong and yet feels so right… zero makes the mathematics hard. Any small event that could potentially become recordable will take you away from your goal. You are asking people to hide data that could potentially be incredibly valuable to your organization.

When we say we can achieve zero, we must be clear on what type of events are included in our zero calculation; not doing so will eventually lead to unintended consequences. When we fail to be clear, we set unachievable expectations for our teams. Companies often create posters, slogans, and company swag that read, "Our goal is zero." Employees wear the article of clothing and are taught to repeat such phrases without understanding what they are telling their teams. This leads to employees roaming hallways, production facilities, operations centers, and company footprints, jumping from issue to issue while missing what really matters: high-risk actions that could cause significant harm.

Humans are fallible, and it's only a matter of time until failure creeps up through your organization and a serious event takes place. Our goal as leaders is to recognize that failure will occur; in fact, we must plan for failures to happen and institute controls that allow them to fail safely. Failing safely is what allows us to keep our people safe; failing safely should be the only way to look at life. Failing safely is a way of accepting the truth but not allowing that truth of failure to lead to an unsafe outcome.

I attended Amphi Middle School in Tucson, Arizona, and I vividly recall the high ropes course at the school gym. We were strapped to a harness that allowed us to climb to the top of the course, where students would navigate through a set of obstacles that included nets, wire crossings, and even a platform where only the bravest of students would attempt to jump over to a trapeze-like contraption. Those who made it finished the course, while those who came up short (which happened far more often) would be "saved" by the harness system. The intent of the course was never to have everyone succeed at the jump but to allow failures to occur. It's the same reason modern vehicles are built with so many safety features: **people will fail**, and those layers of protection exist to keep us safe when we do. Today's cars include brake-assist systems, lane-keeping alerts, blind-spot indicators, collision warnings, and an ever-growing array of sensors and cameras—all designed to notify the driver when they're drifting toward danger. These tools don't replace human judgment; they reinforce it. They create a margin for error, catch what we miss, and step in when our attention slips. In the same way, the systems, processes, and protections we build into our work environment are meant to support people at their most human moments, when mistakes are most likely to occur.

How can your employees fail safely? What layers of protection need to be put in place around work activities to limit the most severe harm? Are we looking at low-probability, high-consequence events with a keen eye for safety, or are we ignoring such events simply because they haven't happened before? When companies fail to see risk in this manner, they fail to capture the devastating impact it will have on their organizations.

At a board meeting for one of the companies I worked at, I was once asked if zero incidents were achievable. It was an urgent moment for the company, and it was the question no one wanted to answer. It was difficult to give a satisfactory response; it's easier to say something like, "It's aspirational," or "With enough time, we can almost certainly achieve it." These phrases may work in media circles, public meetings, or even motivational speeches, but they rarely hold up in reality.

As leaders, we have to be bold enough to face these questions and follow them with actions grounded in trust and understanding. Eyes around the room met mine as I answered plainly, "No—what incidents are we trying to prevent?"

I could tell the room did not like the answer I gave, but they were intrigued by my approach to the question. In an effort to gain consensus that all incidents were indeed preventable, the board chair asked another board member, "John, what do you think of William's answer?"

The room was silent for a moment as all eyes turned toward John. It felt like the room was eagerly waiting for him to disagree with me and return to the line of thinking the board was comfortable with. But John carried a different kind of authority into that room, earned in an industry where margins for error are razor thin and consequences are unforgiving. Captain John M. Cox is one of the most respected safety and risk minds in aviation: a retired airline captain with more than 14,000 flight hours who went on to found Safety Operating Systems (SOS), a firm that helps organizations build safety management systems, prepare for crises, and investigate incidents with the same discipline that keeps airliners safe at 35,000 feet. Over decades, he has studied the hard lessons of aviation—what happens when systems fray, when assumptions go unchallenged, and when weak signals are ignored. He has been called into the aftermath of serious events, including fatal accidents, to help leaders face the truth, honor the people affected, and rebuild the kind of culture where safety isn't a slogan—it's a daily practice.

Instead of pushing back, Captain Cox leaned forward and drew from a lifetime of operating and analyzing risk in a high-consequence industry. In a deep and steady voice, he answered, "I absolutely agree with William's answer, and I'll prove why. It is perfectly okay for the wings of an airplane to fall off in mid-flight, as long as it is less probable than 10^{-9} per flight hour."

John had completely seized the room. With that simple answer, he had made his point, and he had made it well.

It is impossible for companies to design an airplane that will never fatigue, fail, or experience issues in flight. In aviation, the goal is not perfection for an endless amount of time. Instead, the goal is to define tolerable risk and ensure planes are retired before they reach those limits. The goal is redundancy, allowing failures to occur while ensuring the backup system takes over. And in the commercial aviation industry, redundancy goes beyond backup systems. Airlines even consider supply chain redundancy: ensuring that two critical components that serve as "backups" for each other don't come from the same batch or source, thereby reducing the probability that both pieces of equipment share the same failure mechanism.

With that mindset switch, company mantras went from "Our goal is zero" to "Our goal is risk reduction." It took us from treating every event the same way, regardless of size or risk, to focusing on what truly mattered: the hazards that were hurting our people, the controls that would stop them, and the leadership courage required to make safety real.

REFRAMING RISK

When we say that every injury must be prevented, we cripple our organizations by telling them to look at each type of event exactly the same, without recognizing that doing so will keep our focus away from what we were really trying to avoid at the beginning: a serious injury or fatality that will have detrimental and enduring impacts on the company and, more importantly, the lives of our people. In no way do we ignore any event, but we must recognize the tolerable risks we can bear versus those that require immediate action. Caring for our teams and organization means focusing on what truly matters.

We must prepare ourselves for the tough decisions and changes that companies need. While it is important to maintain certain cultural norms that allow us to be successful, we must also understand the challenges we must face head-on to change the thinking of our businesses. Changing our view of risk allowed me to focus our company on the most valuable programs and strategies to reduce risk, leading to a safer, more focused approach to our business.

If you're a parent, you understand this concept well. We accept small risks like a scraped knee, and we aim to keep the child from more serious injuries. We teach children important lessons, such as looking both ways before they cross the road or not talking to strangers, because we know the risks associated with not learning these life lessons could be detrimental.

The same should hold true in the workplace. At each company I've had the pleasure to work for, when we got rid of the myth of zero risk, risk reduction became a way of life. We began walking a path toward ensuring all decisions revolved around continuous improvement and risk reduction. Our employees began thinking about risk differently in their everyday activities, challenging each other to look at their work and work sites for what could go wrong. They adopted a focused approach to the things that could get them hurt, helping each other stay safe and making meaningful changes in the way work was started, performed, and finished each day. We started making risk-informed financial decisions and focusing our attention on the critical areas where risk could be most effectively mitigated through the available resources and funding. The culture started to change, and we began seeing progress that we had never experienced before. Safety was no longer achieved by a whack-a-mole mentality that felt cozy in executive meetings; it was a targeted approach that was tangible and meaningful.

PREPARATION LEADS TO INNOVATION

Preparing the horse for battle means doing our part to train ourselves to make the difficult changes that are needed. This requires us to do all that we can to make decisions that will serve our company best, realizing that challenges will come and difficult situations will be encountered. We can't prevent every issue, but we can understand that our risk mitigation strategies can help us reduce preventable situations. Every day, I prepare for battle. I wake up thinking about what must be done: *How do we grow as a team? How do we get better? How do we stay ready? How do we make sure we're teaching others to be prepared?* Preparing the horse for battle is about doing our part long before the real test arrives. It means training ourselves to make the difficult changes required, making decisions that serve the company's long-term health, and acknowledging that challenges will come. We can't eliminate every issue, but we can build strong risk-mitigation practices that reduce preventable events and strengthen our ability to respond. Leaders train with the expectation that we will win, not by accident but because preparation has become our daily discipline.

This approach brought us to a place where meaningful change was happening in our business model. Once zero risk wasn't the goal, we were free to focus on the toughest and most challenging problems that had been skipped over for many years. A notable example of this was our work around the modeling of pipeline risk, which had traditionally been performed with spreadsheets and simple calculations. We moved to advancing our geospatial information platforms and digital maps of our assets. We developed probabilistic risk models that painted a more accurate picture of where we needed to move resources and dollars to reduce the most risk within our infrastructure improvement plans. Within occupational safety, we looked at our data and found ways to keep our employees safer by improving our processes and procedures while keeping in mind that people are fallible and will make mistakes. This led us to understand human errors better so that we could provide them with tools and technology that would help them fail safely when performing critical work.

The improvements were obvious to the leadership team, but they were also felt by the employees. Teams weren't being bombarded by an overwhelming amount of information and changes; we were targeting the right things at the right time.

To achieve this, we focused on what mattered most. We prepared our employees to understand where they needed to focus their time and attention, and they were prepared to walk the journey alongside the leadership team. People were invigorated by the fact that they had a focus and weren't being pulled in many directions.

THE IMPORTANCE OF PREPARATION AND PERSISTENT DEDICATION

As leaders, we are ultimately responsible for the actions of our teams, and we must strive to address all known threats in a safe and repeatable manner. That's how we prepare. We understand what's in front of us, seek counsel, and make decisions, sometimes faster than anticipated.

We can never control all results, but we must do our part to understand and control what we can. As a young leader, it frustrated me when things didn't go as I planned. I struggled to accept when things went wrong, even when my team and I were giving our best. Eventually, I learned to see these failures in a different light.

Early in my career, one of my assignments as a junior engineer was to perform a yearly calibration of all the gas lines being built around the world by my company, as well as competitors, and predict when the best time was to introduce new pipelines. The task was complex but manageable: research world economics and politics, interview experts to feed the industry gas outlook model, and present the findings to senior leaders. The impact of the yearly study would allow billions of dollars to be adequately placed within the short- and long-range financial plans, impacting permitting, budgeting, financing, engineering, design, and so much more.

In my research, I learned that some pipelines would span bodies of water while others would cross mountain regions and valleys. As I worked on this project, I was reminded of just how small the world is. Envisioning where these pipelines would traverse the earth reminded me of spinning the globe as a kid, marveling at the landmasses that make up our world.

I was thrilled to do a job that was valued by the company and could make a difference. I loved it so much that I would arrive at 5 a.m. and often leave at 8 p.m., driven by a desire to learn more. After everyone else had left for the day, my leader, Jan, would often come and ask me if I had any questions. He had run the project for many years and understood the modeling software better than most.

During the finalization of the model, I noticed that my answers didn't align with what was expected. I was giving it my best, but my results weren't showing it. Late one night, while Jan and I were both scratching our heads, I noticed that the model's calculations were not in alignment with what I had been taught by previous model users.

We quickly realized that the model was wrong, and it had been wrong for years! Since no one had questioned it, the same model had been used year after year. Mark my words, you will hear the following phrase throughout your careers: "It's the way we've always done it." This phrase is a natural part of any leadership journey, but I learned an important lesson that day: preparation and persistent dedication can make a lasting impact. Without Jan's help and patience, I would have thought my preparation and hard work were in vain. Instead, I learned the value of doing my best regardless of the outcome.

Finding the error in the industry gas outlook algorithm led us to recalibrate our program and strategy and look more deeply at our practices and processes. These changes led to better decisions all year round for our pipeline projects worldwide. I learned the important lesson of preparing the horse and equipping it with all that was needed for battle: its armor, its training, and its nourishment. But I also learned that what comes after may be out of our control. The win was in knowing we did everything possible.

PERFECTION ISN'T THE GOAL

My encouragement to all leaders is that there's no time to waste. Today is the day to understand that you will not be perfect at what you do; you will have obstacles to face, and often, it may seem as though failure occurred in spite of arduous preparation.

Our job is not to control every external force but to understand the threats around us, put controls in place to mitigate them, and take responsibility for learning from every outcome, especially when the result isn't what we hoped for. Outcomes matter. They tell us whether our assumptions were right and where our systems fell short.

It's our responsibility to prepare ourselves and our teams as thoroughly as possible, and then, at times, to hold outcomes with humility, not dismissing them but recognizing that even when we do things right, the result may still surprise us. What matters is that we stay nimble, learn quickly, and adjust our approach, ready to respond to new challenges as they arise and continue to grow and improve.

Things may never be perfect, the risk may never be zero, and plans may fall through. However, our preparation helps us navigate those situations and create a healthy culture for our teams in the process. Our preparation helps us recover faster than other companies, and it ensures that we handle changes with integrity and trust.

This type of preparation makes us resilient to changing conditions. It allows us to bring reason and hope to tough situations as we weather through problems one challenge at a time. Our preparation makes us an asset to companies; we become the individuals who can be trusted when things get tough. When everyone is sinking, we are ready to provide first aid to those in need and point to a way out. I encourage you to find ways to prepare yourself and your team for battles. Some battles may be small, while others will test every skill and strength you have. Practice this each day, and you will find yourself more resilient. In fact, you will thrive when challenges occur.

History shows us the weight of that responsibility, but we fulfill it by building a legacy rooted in the well-being of our people, which we explore next.

GET TO WORK:

1. Write down three early career experiences that shaped how you approach safety, people, or leadership today. Identify one lesson from each that you actively apply or should apply in your current role.

2. Assess your team's or company's response to past setbacks or failures. Pinpoint one process, behavior, or mindset that needs to change to ensure you're learning and improving, not repeating history.

3. Define the legacy you want to lead. Write one sentence that captures the culture you want to build, then identify one specific action you can take this week to reinforce that vision.

4. Define what an acceptable risk is and why it is acceptable. This is a formal process with a written risk assessment, evaluation of mitigations, and acceptance by leadership.

2

GROUND YOURSELF ON WHAT MATTERS

"Be sure you know the condition of your flocks, give careful attention to your herds; for riches do not endure forever, and a crown is not secure for all generations."
Proverbs 27:23–24 NIV

The opening verse is a timeless reminder that leadership is not meant to be distant. Knowing the condition of your people requires showing up, listening without filters, and staying close to where the work is actually being done. You cannot lead well from a conference room alone or measure culture from a spreadsheet. When leaders drift too far from their people, they begin to manage numbers instead of serving human beings. Titles fade, profits fluctuate, and roles change, but people carry the culture forward long after leaders are gone. When we place people first, when we "follow the trucks," we protect what truly sustains an organization. That is how trust is built, purpose is restored, and a legacy takes root that no title or crown could ever secure.

During my more than twenty-five years in the oil and gas industry, I have witnessed a variety of different leaders and leadership styles. Success looks different from leader to leader, with some putting more emphasis on safety, innovation, efficiency, or overall marketplace performance. When leaders emphasize only one of these factors, it often leads to an unbalanced approach to leadership, which does not allow a positive legacy to grow within the work environment. The best leaders, those who leave lasting positive legacies, are able to balance all of these components within a business, even in times of hardship and challenges. The best leaders understand what is needed across the business and meet their responsibilities without sacrificing their core values and what really matters.

I first encountered the concept of "following the trucks" during one of my first tasks after joining Pacific Gas and Electric Company. I was to separate our engineering department into two distinct groups: one group to support extensive field activities alongside field operations, and another to focus on engineering designs. There was a talented young man named Scott who sat right across from me. He was bright, highly knowledgeable in his field, and, especially as a new employee, someone I quickly learned I could trust. He had been with the company for some time and was always generous with his experience, willing to teach and guide me whenever I had questions.

As I began reorganizing my department, I saw Scott as someone I wanted on my new team. I had already planned a conversation with him about the opportunity when he surprised me with a perspective that would leave a lasting impression. During our discussion, he said, "William, I'd love to work for you, but over the years, I've learned to follow the trucks."

I chuckled and asked him what he meant. Scott explained that he had come to realize how much he valued being close to the people who actually carried out the work every day. To him, "following the trucks" meant staying connected to where the real work happens and remaining close enough to see reality as it is, not as it's filtered through layers of reporting. He believed that staying near the front lines ensured he never lost sight of what truly mattered.

I found it hard to argue with him. His reasoning was thoughtful, practical, and humbling. In the end, I respected his decision and wished him well, knowing he was choosing the place where he felt he could make the greatest impact.

Over time, I came to fully appreciate the wisdom in Scott's words. By following the trucks, leaders gain true speed to knowledge—the advantage of seeing issues, barriers, and emerging risks before they become tomorrow's crisis or next month's report. When you stay close to the work, you hear the truth sooner, see problems firsthand, and can remove obstacles before they slow the team down. Few leaders ever experience this vantage point, yet it is one of the most powerful ways to stay informed, connected, and effective.

Looking back, this lesson from Scott profoundly shaped my leadership approach. Even though he was younger than me, he taught me an essential truth: the best leaders never drift too far from where the work occurs.

Consider your own business; maybe you run a clinic. Have you forgotten to visit the front line, where the nurses and staff work? Or perhaps you work for Amazon, Uber, or Lyft. Have you talked to the drivers to understand their challenges?

I remind my team of this principle regularly, especially when facing challenges. I ask, "Are you following the trucks? Are you engaging with the team on the ground? Are you aware of their struggles? Do you know their names, their families, and what they are going through?"

Now, in my construction-driven business, I find joy in getting out into the field, learning from my colleagues, mentoring them, and understanding their challenges firsthand. This insight cannot be easily gathered through employee engagement surveys or phone calls; it's obtained by being present with the people doing the work.

We must recognize that we will not always see all of our success within the time we are in a specific role or even during our time with the company. Instead, through our leadership, we can place the building blocks in the appropriate places so that future leaders can reap the rewards. The leader who thinks only about what they will gain tomorrow misses the real opportunities to build sustainable change that will stand the test of time. Those leaders who can make incremental changes over prolonged periods of time have greater potential to lead a lasting legacy.

The timeless recipe that produces outstanding results is quite simple. In fact, it only has two ingredients: people and safety.

When we are able to recognize the importance of placing people and safety at the heart of everything we do, we will more abundantly enjoy the work we do while enhancing employee engagement, creating a legacy we can be proud to leave behind.

WHY ARE PEOPLE THE GREATEST ASSET?

Like any good recipe, order matters. In the recipe for good leadership, people always come first. Leaders who focus on people first will ultimately achieve better results and have a greater opportunity to accomplish all of the performance metrics the company aspires to achieve.

This isn't just a nice idea, but it is backed up by data. A 2023 Forbes article titled "People

First: A Framework for Modern Leaders" points to surveys that indicate that a people-first mindset results in "twenty-two percent higher productivity, forty-one percent lower absenteeism, and thirty percent stronger customer satisfaction." These are impressive statistics that provide a glimpse into some of the benefits associated with placing our people first. Still, there's so much more to a people-first mindset than what the company gets in return.

A study by McKinsey found that "seventy percent of employees said that their sense of purpose is defined by their work. So, like it or not, as a company leader, you play an important part in helping your employees find their purpose and live it. And you have your work cut out: our survey also found disparities in how frontline employees and other groups feel supported—or thwarted—in living their purpose at work."

Even more striking, seventy percent of those surveyed stated that their sense of purpose is largely defined by work. Out of nearly one thousand employees surveyed, eighty-five percent of executives or upper management expressed that they were living their purpose, but only fifteen percent of frontline employees felt the same way.

Leaders must have a keen understanding of what their people need. We also need to grasp what barriers need to be removed to allow individuals to find joy and purpose at work. Frontline employees need to feel valued and appreciated, and this can only happen when we lead with a conviction to place our people first in all our decisions.

We must recognize that the gauge for a healthy organization cannot be how we feel as a leadership group. In fact, this can be a distraction at work. Leaders receive good feedback from their bosses, and they quickly interpret this as success, but this could be the very feedback that will prevent us from placing people first. Our responsibility is to dig deeper into our organization to find what our employees need. It's our privilege to meet employees' needs, ensure they feel valued, and make decisions with their best interests in mind.

For most of your career, you will find yourself in one of two environments. Either you will work under unbalanced leadership that focuses primarily on top-line metrics (often financial) or under leaders who start with people and then measure everything else that matters.

In the first scenario, the leadership team judges results by measures of success that have little to do with the people. In this situation, you are responsible for going beyond these metrics to be successful. You will need to place an even greater value on people to ensure that the temporary success you are experiencing can be maintained. Leaders who care intentionally for their people are not forgotten. In the second scenario, the more balanced leadership wants to know how the people are doing, what they are experiencing day to day, and what they need to be successful. Key metrics are still driven each day, but only once a people and safety culture is secured. More often than not, these are the leaders who have successful, sustainable, and high-performing teams. These are the leaders who are remembered.

Remember: leaders come and go, but great leaders lead a legacy because they recognize it's about our people. When we care about our people, our entire vernacular changes. When we place people first, we don't allow any decision to proceed without it being vetted through the people-first filter. We ask inquisitive questions to test whether or not our employees are placing our people first. We challenge norms and seek feedback from those who know best: our people. In a people-first culture, we roam the halls of our buildings with gratitude, not attempting to find fault or just point to problems, but praising the work our employees are doing. By no means does this mean we don't coach or fix issues; it simply means we start by seeing the good our people bring to the table first. When we speak, joy overflows, and we can't wait to encourage the next employee. This isn't a lack of performance management; a good leader understands that balance and finds ways to help employees bring their best to work.

Placing people first is all about being there for our employees without expecting anything back. It's about making a fundamental shift from what we want to what they need. It's about walking the floors of our company, hearing from our employees, lifting them up, and removing barriers across departments.

Corporate America teaches us from day one to watch over profit margins, asset integrity, data-driven results, and more. While this type of leadership can deliver on portions of the business, it can only go so far. If people aren't the primary focus, we will never be able to realize the full potential of the business. For so many leaders, learning the key principles about people first comes too late.

It's easy to forget that our people are the most powerful tool we have to understand what is going on around us. They are the best real-time culture surveys and provide the timeliest feedback on what is going well and what is not. From administrative assistants who support us to the janitors who keep our buildings clean to every single field and office employee who takes a pulse on our culture, people are the bloodline of business.

Each person in our business plays a role, and when we can engage everyone, we gain valuable insight into what's happening and what may come. Once trust is built, each individual in our company plays a significant role in shaping and molding the culture of the environments where we lead.

Every person is important. Regardless of their title or department, each employee has valuable insight into how we can make things better. It's a leader's responsibility to know this and care for their teams each and every day.

Leaders who learn this early are able to break down problems and assess the most valuable opportunities to support their organizations. The closer we can get to those performing the work at the front lines, the closer we can get to the heart of our company culture.

TOOLS TO HELP KEEP PEOPLE FIRST

At this point, you may be wondering how to put the principle of "putting people first" into practice. Here are some common practices and tools that have helped me gain valuable insight into my people. Applying these to my teams has helped me stay focused on what matters most, even as my title has moved me further from the trucks.

Win-Train-Send

I have shared this simple formula with my leaders as we bring people to our companies. I start by helping all leaders understand that we aren't here to hire employees; we are here to win the best employees for the company, instilling a sense of passion and belonging like no other.

Once we win our people, our job as leaders is to train them and provide the resources they need to be successful. It's vital that we spend the time investing in people; if our teams aren't successful, then the company can't be.

One of the greatest engagement tools is to send our team members off to be our next leaders and technical experts based on their aspirations and skills. This is one way that we can lead a legacy. We pour into our leaders so that they can pour into others, no matter what company or industry they find themselves in next.

Win, Train, Send is a continuous cycle. Once we go through one cycle with our employees, it's our trigger to start the cycle once again. We win them to the company every day through our leadership. We should constantly be winning them, training them, and sending them off to continue to grow within the company.

Field Visits

I have made it my passion to visit those closest to the work. I do this by scheduling regular field visits to meet with employees and listen to them. During these field visits, I ask what I can do to support them and what tools they need to be successful. These visits often provide quick wins and help build trust, opening the door for continued engagement. The world-renowned car manufacturer, Toyota, calls these walks Gemba Walks, a lean management strategy that encourages leaders to visit the place where work is occurring in order to gain a firsthand view of opportunities for improvements, ultimately leading to waste reduction and increased efficiency.

No matter your industry or the size of your organization, you can begin implementing this today. Who are the people on the front lines? Make it a point to meet with them regularly, not to assess their performance or inform them of some change, but to listen. Then, take what you learned and act on it. If a frontline employee needs a better tool to complete a task, work to provide that for them. If a policy needs to be changed, begin exploring what that looks like.

Remember that people are the most important part of any organization. When people are cared for, everyone wins. Listening to employees' needs, engaging meaningfully with them, and acting on their feedback goes a long way toward creating a people-first culture.

Coffee Chats

I love my coffee chats with my teams! These "all-hands" calls are an opportunity for unfiltered feedback on how we are doing. At one point, one of my coffee chats had approximately one thousand invites!

When employees realized they had an open forum to share their thoughts and that leadership was not filtering questions, they were eager to share. We answered all of their questions, both tough and easy ones, and the coffee chats became a place to recognize employees, champion the department's success, and work together to fix our problems.

We need to create opportunities where employees can openly ask questions without being filtered. These types of forums contribute to a culture of openness and honesty and help employees feel valued. I also want to encourage you to constantly look for opportunities to keep people first. One of my favorite examples comes from a CEO friend of mine from an electric and gas utility company. During the construction of their new corporate headquarters, he was asked whether the executive offices should face the parking lot or the more scenic view, and he was crystal clear about his decision. He asked that the executive office face the parking lot, allowing employees to enjoy the more pleasant view of the surrounding landscape. This small decision rippled through the company and had a positive impact on employee engagement.

KEEPING PEOPLE FIRST

Placing people first is more than simply being nice or being a good team player. This principle requires us to understand our people and help them achieve their goals and aspirations. It's about caring enough for those who give themselves to work each day and showing that care in our actions and speech.

I've been blessed to watch utility workers for over twenty-five years "run to the problems." When there is an emergency, they sacrifice their time with family to fix the problems at hand. I witnessed this after the San Bruno, CA, and the Merrimack Valley incident in Massachusetts. In both instances, the employees rallied together to respond to the emergency and rebuild those communities. Behind the scenes, I felt the passion employees had for reshaping organizational cultures to ensure that events like those would never happen again.

Internally, we had created a culture that put people first. When our employees were cared for, they were excited to go above and beyond for those in the communities we served. In little and big ways, each member of those teams focused on what mattered, and in the face of tragedy, that care made all the difference.

Years ago, I met a colleague at work through our leadership development program. She had recently returned to the workforce and was ecstatic about working with people and helping them grow in their roles. As we talked, she was excited to tell me the story of what she had gone through over the last few years. Behind her smile and passion, which radiated from her like a light in a dark room, was an individual who had battled cancer and had won. She shared her story with joy and expressed that she would not allow days to dissolve into infinity without value or direction; she had made a decision that life was too precious and that she would take every minute and fill it with something good.

That's how we should feel as leaders. We have been given a chance to lead the easy, the hard, and even the tough-to-reach employees. With the title of leader, we have an opportunity to listen and help fix problems. Each day is an opportunity to put people first and keep them first. After all, without the people, who are you leading? Without people, there's no need for leadership.

If you want to lead a legacy, create spaces to develop and grow your team so that the legacy you leave behind is one that continues to reproduce itself through them.

BUILDING A PEOPLE-FIRST LEGACY: THE HEART OF LEADERSHIP AND TEACHING

When I reflect on the idea of leading a people-first legacy, there is one example that stands above all others: my father. His unwavering commitment to placing people at the center of his work has been the foundation of his life, and it has left a profound mark on everyone he's touched. It's through his actions, his everyday dedication to serving and caring for others, that I've come to understand what true leadership and legacy are all about.

There are three things that have connected my father and me throughout my life: a shared love for Christ, a passion for cars, and a deep respect for work and the people who give themselves each day to do a great job. Watching him navigate the challenges and triumphs of his career has shaped so much of who I am today as a husband, father, friend, employee, and leader. But the most powerful lessons came not from what he said but from what he did.

I had the privilege of witnessing my father's leadership in real-time from a young age, as he helped to run sustainable logging programs in the rugged, remote areas near Darien, Panama. I watched as he and my mother made the courageous decision to leave behind everything they knew to give our family a new life in the United States. I saw him lead with grace, humility, and pride as he managed his fleet team at the University of Arizona. These experiences gave me a front-row seat to a leadership style that was built on care, respect, and an unshakable belief that people are the most important part of any endeavor.

WHAT DOES A "PEOPLE-FIRST" LEGACY LOOK LIKE?

A people-first legacy isn't about titles or accolades. It's about the impact you have on those around you and how you elevate others, empowering them to grow and succeed. Leadership, when done right, is about developing others, not just managing them. It's about teaching, mentoring, and serving in ways that help others reach their full potential.

I've seen this in my father's work as well as in how he led every aspect of his life. One morning when I was learning to drive, my father took me to a remote dirt road southwest of Tucson, near the Kitt Peak National Observatory. He chose the roughest, most challenging terrain he could find: a bumpy, washboard road full of rocks and ruts that would test both me and the car. For hours, he taught me how to control the car, use the clutch properly, understand the instrument gauges, and safely navigate obstacles. He created an environment that would prepare for almost any situation. After many lessons, I became the kid who, from a young age, could drive almost anything; if it had a steering wheel, I could maneuver it, and if an issue happened mechanically, I was taught to listen and act to fix it. It was grueling and sometimes frustrating, but it was also one of the most meaningful experiences of my life. I will cherish those days forever, and as I look back now, I can reminisce with him about how valuable that time was for me and my growth. Over many months, the lessons continued, each time teaching me something new about driving, each time showing me how much he cared.

He taught me this way because he cared deeply for my safety, growth, and success. He could have enrolled me in a traditional driver's education program, but instead, he created an environment where I could learn by doing, where I could fail safely and learn from my mistakes. And most importantly, he showed me through his actions that he cared about me, not just as his son, but as a person who deserved the best of his attention and guidance.

My father's approach to teaching wasn't limited to just me. Throughout his career, he treated everyone with the same level of respect, care, and commitment. Whether he was training employees at the University of Arizona's fleet/shuttle program, coaching his team to be better drivers, or at church alongside my mother helping others through troubled marriages and broken homes, his focus was always on people. He didn't just manage tasks; he invested in people's lives, listening to their needs and offering guidance when necessary. Even years after his retirement, employees continue to seek his advice. That's the kind of legacy my father built, one where people matter more than anything else.

A Lifelong Learner and Teacher

One key to my father's constant drive to grow and help others is his passion for learning. My father has never stopped learning. He has never stopped asking questions, seeking new ways to improve, or finding opportunities to pass on his wisdom to others. Even as he enjoys the well-earned rest of retirement, he is still fully invested in the success of others, especially his children and our families.

To this day, he reaches out to check in on me and asks me how my role as a senior leader is progressing. "How are you taking care of your people?" he'll ask. "What else can you do to improve?" These aren't just casual questions. These are the questions of a man who still sees leadership as a lifelong mission that doesn't end with a title or retirement.

For my father, the work of developing and caring for people doesn't stop. He's always pushing me to think about how I can continue to be better, how I can keep improving, and how I can keep lifting others along the way. His feedback is never about criticism but about helping me see the potential for growth in both myself and my team.

Even in retirement, my father's mind and heart are driven by a desire for continuous improvement. It's a mindset that permeates everything he does, and it's something that he instills in everyone he meets. His care for others is not just about kindness but about helping people be the best versions of themselves. He is a teacher at heart, but he's also a learner, constantly seeking new ways to help others grow, whether through formal mentorship or simple everyday conversations.

Leading a Legacy Built on People

At the heart of every great leader is a commitment to people. My father has left a legacy built not on numbers or goals, but on relationships and care. Make no mistake about it, my father ran a fleet that performed far beyond the goals set forth by the university. His safety, reliability, and affordability numbers were top in the industry, but his focus was always on people. He didn't just lead his team; he built a culture of trust, respect, and mutual support. His impact goes far beyond any metrics or performance reports; his impact is in the lives of the people he helped, mentored, and loved. And it's *because* my father put people first that he was able to deliver a top-performing program.

This is the challenge I want to present to all of us as leaders, whether in our families, communities, or businesses: Do you know your people? Are you spending time walking the halls, listening to their needs, and understanding their challenges? Are they following you because you have a title or because they know you genuinely care?

A people-first legacy isn't about being perfect or achieving every goal. It's about creating a culture—a foundation where people feel seen, heard, and valued—where they can grow, thrive, and reach their full potential. It's about investing in others, knowing that your true success as a leader is measured not by what you achieve, but by the lives you touch.

As I reflect on my father's life, I am reminded of the profound power of a people-first approach. The legacy he has left isn't just about the fleet program or the work he did; it's about the people he served, mentored, and inspired along the way. That is a legacy that will never fade, and it's one that I strive to carry forward every day.

That's what true leadership looks like. People are where we should always start, and doing this will lay the foundation for success in every other part of life.

GET TO WORK:

1. Use a people-first filter throughout all your decisions: listen, remove barriers, and support their success.
2. Balance metrics with meaning. Yes, metrics matter, but don't let them overshadow what really drives performance: your people, safety, and values.
3. Build for what comes after you. Focus on long-term impact. The legacy you leave is built by the choices you make today, even if the results come later.

3

WITHOUT A VISION, PEOPLE PERISH

"Where there is no vision, the people perish..."
Proverbs 29:18 KJV

W hen we moved from Panama to the United States in 1988, both of my parents became janitors for the University of Arizona. While over time, they were able to advance in their roles, it was a difficult adjustment for them, who had left great jobs behind: my father was a project evaluator for a bank, and my mother was an administrative assistant at the cultural arts department. But they came to the United States with a vision, and nothing would stop that vision from becoming a reality.

My mother left Panama and went from being a well-respected administrative assistant to one of the lowest starting positions at the university. But she did not allow this change to define who she was or limit the impact she could have on others. Instead, she gave her best every day, putting pride into her work and giving back to the people she encountered. She held a clear vision for her future: to work in accounting, the field she had studied in college. While serving faithfully in her role as a janitor, she put in the effort required to advance toward that goal. Along the way, she helped others, both in and out of the workplace, pursue their own dreams.

It took my mother nine long years to fulfill her vision of working in accounting. Throughout that time, she treated everyone around her with respect and dignity, giving back to university staff and students through her commitment to the people she met each day.

My parents' vision required real sacrifice, and it did not materialize overnight. It took years of patient, faithful work before they reached their dreams. Yet even in the waiting, they served those around them, leading a lasting legacy within the university and their community. Their story continues to remind me of the importance of vision; without it, people perish.

COMMUNICATING THE VISION IN GOOD TIMES AND BAD

Vision is always important, but during a crisis, it becomes vital to everything we do. In the workplace, this doesn't mean that we change our vision during difficult times; instead, we must figure out how to communicate the vision clearly as we speak to employees.

When a company is going through a rough patch, that same vision may need to be defined with more detail through the recovery period. Once a steady state is achieved, we may be better positioned to describe the vision with different details that speak to sustainability. Speaking to employees about sustainable outcomes too quickly may not allow them to understand the importance of the actions we are taking in the short term. Even when you are doing your best, sooner or later, you will be called upon to fix something. We need to always be ready as individuals, as a team, and as a company.

Therefore, it is critical that we interpret and share this vision with our teams with an acute understanding of where employees and the company are in their journey.

In the midst of a difficult situation, employees need to understand that we will be able to come out on the other side successfully; while under steady-state operations, we must paint a vision that we are focused on what matters to achieve our desired goals. Regardless of the situation, we must be crystal clear about what we need to achieve and how we will ask our employees to join us on this journey.

VISION THROUGH AN EMPLOYEE'S EYES

Each company I've worked for has, without fail, introduced or revised its mission, vision, and values statement. Revising these essential components of a business has become a natural step for incoming CEOs who hope to leave their stamp on the company's history. Although mission, vision, and values are all essential, vision is the most talked about by employees. It is also the component that has the greatest point of connection for frontline employees.

Any time I've had the opportunity to lead a new department, I have consistently heard employees ask, "What's our vision for the company?" followed by, "Where are we going?" People need to know where a company is in achieving its goals. More importantly, employees need to know how it will embark on what lies ahead.

When an employee asks about the vision, it's likely that they're not asking for a recitation of the company's mission, vision, and values. Instead, they are asking, "Where is the company going? And what does it mean for me?"

For the remainder of this chapter, let's place our conventional thinking of vision aside and see vision more simply. Vision is an invitation for our employees to understand four fundamental principles:

- What they are working toward
- What they are doing to make a difference
- How they are impacted
- How they will lead a legacy

When our employees ask about the company's vision, they are really asking how the company will help them achieve their legacy. Our employees are asking us to paint a vision that they can understand, support, and communicate. They aren't asking us for complex words or cute phrases; they are asking us for clarity that can be utilized at the morning coffee station, casual discussions with peers, and at the dinner table with their significant others. We can all remember the time-less John F. Kennedy story and the janitor at the NASA head-quarters. While touring the facility for the first time, President Kennedy introduced himself to the janitor who was mopping the floors, asking, "What do you do here?" and the janitor replied, "Mr. President, I'm helping put a man on the moon." Kennedy and his team had painted a vision, and that vision had rippled through the walls of NASA, touching every employee.

Like my parents, he was proud to be part of something much bigger.

Imagine this: on the trim line of Toyota's plant in Georgetown, Kentucky, the line is roaring; cars inch forward on the conveyor, every second measured, every motion chore-ographed. In the middle of that rhythm, an assembly-line worker notices something that doesn't look quite right with a single seatbelt fitting. She could ignore it and let it slide to keep the line moving. Instead, she reaches up and pulls the andon cord, the bright rope that any worker is empowered to pull, and the entire line begins to slow, then stops. Team members rush to her station to trace the problem, fix the defect, and only then let the line start again. Later, when she's asked why she would halt a billion-dollar production line for one small part, she doesn't talk about quotas or schedules. She simply says, "I don't like to let something like that go. That's really important for the people who buy our cars." In her mind, she's not just installing hardware—she's protecting the families who will trust their lives to that seatbelt.[1]

---

1. Schifferes, S. "The triumph of lean production." *BBC News*, February 27,

Now that's powerful!

In my own journey in the utility business, I've tried to see and honor that same spirit in our frontline employees. They are utility workers, and as one mentor of mine said, they represent one of the last standing true American trades. They help construct and maintain the infrastructure that runs across this country, carrying electrons and molecules to homes, businesses, and now to some of the largest energy-consuming technologies being introduced through AI and global modernization. These men and women wake up to work during rain or shine, all while making sure customers receive the utmost care and that service is restored as soon as practicable and always in a safe manner.

I've tried to make sure our employees see the importance of what they do, the value they bring, and that they understand they are performing work that is an absolute necessity to the world. When utility workers really grasp this, they show up with a passion unlike anything I've ever seen: they come ready to help their communities, and they can literally see their purpose come to life. Over many years, I've watched residents come out of their homes to bring cookies, hang handmade signs, and sometimes almost hold little parades with their kids to thank our crews for restoring power and gas service. Most people probably don't realize it, but those moments fill the hearts of our workers. Even after long hours and hard days, they are rejuvenated, energized, and ready to do it again because they know their work matters. And just like the vision JFK cast for that NASA janitor, that is exactly

2007. http://news.bbc.co.uk/2/hi/business/6346315.stm.

what we want to see today: stories like these modeled again and again, and leaders who do everything they can to bring those stories to life so every employee understands their purpose, is proud of it, and can live each day knowing that wherever they are in the company, they are fulfilling a purpose that will lead a legacy.

Instead of spending considerable time in this book focusing on the process of establishing a company vision statement, I want to offer a distinct perspective. As leaders, we have learned how to develop solid vision statements that can be used globally throughout the company, and we are typically good at laying this out in a one-page document that gets circulated around our offices and posted on lunchroom corkboards. But there's an aspect of vision that we may be overlooking.

An essential part of vision-casting is carrying the vision to the front line in a basic manner that leaves a lasting impact. If we want our vision to actually take place, we need the employees to buy in. Without them, a vision statement is just a nice thought.

This chapter is not about creating a vision statement; it's about making the vision meaningful to employees. I believe that if we can grasp this concept, we will gain a better understanding of how to translate our company's vision and inspire our employees. Think about vision as a way for employees to grasp not just the long-term vision of the company but also the near-term objectives. Think of vision as a clarifying agent that helps a team work together to achieve the same goals. And when all of the teams are united by a vision, the entire company is energized by a common purpose.

I've participated in strategic discussions where the senior leadership team painted what we thought was a clear picture of how our company was performing, only to realize that our discussions provided little clarity to our employees about our vision. Our vision had been constructed in a way we thought employees would quickly rally around, but that was far from reality. We felt confident in the plan that was laid out, but as we looked deeper, we found that the vision hadn't reached employees who were desperate for direction. Does that sound familiar? Have you put a statement together that sounded energizing, only to find out that employees don't really understand it?

The vision we paint can become one of the most important tools for our employees to understand where we are going and why. A clear vision also gives teams something to rally around as one. Throughout my career leading multidisciplinary groups across the country, I have found that painting a clear vision has allowed me to break down communication barriers and gather around one sustainable strategy. This unobstructed vision invigorates the organization to achieve its goals and objectives year over year.

We cannot simply create a vision, hoping that it will stick. A lasting and effective vision must have employee buy-in and allow us to translate a clear path forward together.

INVITING PEOPLE INTO THE VISION

Our job as leaders is to translate the company's vision to our teams so they can see a clear line of sight, making it tangible and achievable. The most powerful vision statements capture the hearts and minds of our employees and those we have the privilege of serving. These are the vision statements that become ingrained in the DNA of our companies and stand the test of time. They are simple and shy away from words and taglines that can only be understood by fancy consulting firms, upper leadership, and college professors.

What employees need is a simple vision that can help them focus and remain focused. The vision statement for one company I worked for was, "The plan is the plan." This vision was caught by the employees, and they were still reciting it over ten years after it had first been shared. The vision was tied to a period of time when the company needed to drive repeatable practices. When the "plan" was developed, they focused on ensuring that it was held sacred so as to avoid disruption, especially through periods of change.

WITHOUT A VISION, PEOPLE PERISH

As mentioned earlier, when the vision isn't clear, employees are left alone to wonder what leaders are trying to communicate. If there's no end in sight and they have to try to interpret their leaders' meaning, they grow weary. When there is a lack of clear vision, employees begin to think about everything wrong with the company and point back to one widespread problem: there's no vision.

For years, I ensured that the vision was simple and clear for my department. I have taken time to interpret the company's overall vision into something meaningful and tangible for employees, and I invite you to do the same within your own company.

In the utility space, vision statements often boil down to a focus on safety, reliability, and affordability. These are all great starting points, but when we step back, our employees still need to understand how we will get there. Mission and values can help bring some clarity, but they rarely get to the heart of the issue: painting a clear picture for our people.

At every company, I've taken the vision, mission, and values scripted for the organization, and I have helped employees tell the story for the vision (what they're working toward, what they are doing to make a difference, how they are impacted, and how they will lead a legacy). Few things will get people energized about work until we can show them that their actions will have impacts on others, that they, too, can lead a legacy. Instead of just repeating the phrases, I have helped people understand what their legacy will look like if the vision is executed with excellence. That's what our employees need!

I share my insights from a perspective grounded in experience and authority. For twenty-five years I saw consistent patterns in all of the companies I worked on. These patterns pointed me in the direction of a very clear vision for success. I noticed that all of those companies had five things in common that made them successful: people, safety, compliance, quality, and financial stewardship. I simply look for those patterns and build a clear strategy. I urge you to do the same in your company; look for those patterns.

I asked my team to focus on what became our **Five Keys to Success**: people, safety, compliance, quality, and financial stewardship. These were not initiatives or slogans—they became our operating system. They shaped how we made decisions, how we led, how we showed up for one another, and how we measured success. Over time, the Five Keys became embedded in the fabric of our organization, ringing across every level and serving as a shared language and commitment.

At the center of these Five Keys was a remarkably simple and powerful vision: **Place People and Safety First.** I consistently emphasized that the sequence mattered. When we anchored ourselves in people and safety, excellence in compliance, quality, and financial stewardship naturally followed. This clarity created alignment, accountability, and trust. By ensuring every leader and employee understood not just the words but the meaning behind them, the Five Keys became more than a framework—they became who we were as a team, how our vision came to life in the everyday, and how we consistently delivered results with integrity.

Our intentionality in these areas helped set us up to be successful now and into the future. These simple focus areas were always part of the company's vision; I just translated the vision into terms my team could remember and understand. When a leader makes the vision clear, relevant, and action-able for their employees, positive results follow. These words became part of our daily culture, and without thinking twice, thousands of employees started to understand what we were after and how we were going to get there.

What are simple words within your organization that will resonate with your teams? I want to challenge you to find the words your employees need in order to know what is expected of them and how they will achieve their goals.

Below is how I would teach my leaders to walk through these terms with their teams, opening conversations and empowering leaders to tell the why behind the what. I encourage you to think about how you can translate what I have done to your own organization and your teams. Consider the impact you could have on your company or business if people and safety were at the heart of everything you did.

People and Safety

We will place people and safety at the heart of everything we do and make no decision without thinking about them first. We will send our people home to their families and loved ones in the same way they came to work in the morning. We will listen, understand their needs, and remove the barriers they have. We will place our people first, and we will never sacrifice safety. We will be remembered for how we took care of our people and the public; we will never forget this.

Compliance

Compliance is the price of admission. It is foundational, and it is the minimum requirement to operate. It is our privilege to serve the communities in which we live, and we can never take that lightly. Without compliance, we don't have a license to operate. We will always be compliant and will look for opportunities to exceed these minimum expectations.

Quality

We will place quality at the source! The source is our people, and it will always be where we embed quality. We will seek to continuously improve.

Financial Stewardship

We will continue to be good stewards of the dollars we have been entrusted with. We look for ways to enhance processes and drive down costs so we can reinvest back into our people and our business and reduce operational risk while keeping customers' costs as low as reasonably possible.

When I first shared this vision with my teams, it didn't take long for it to become second nature. It rolled off our tongues with clarity and conviction. We knew exactly where we were headed. The energy was palpable; our teams were invigorated, and the message resonated all the way to our frontline employees.

I made it clear: anything that diverted us from this vision would be challenged, tested, and held to account. This wasn't just a slogan; it was a standard. I've applied this simple yet powerful framework across every team I've led, and I encourage others to discover what resonates within their own organizations.

So, what would you have seen if you walked through our offices?

You would have witnessed a culture of intentionality, a team that asked, "Before we make this decision, have we considered how it will impact our employees?" and, "Are we doing this safely, and can we stand behind our choices with integrity?" These weren't just questions; they were guiding principles.

Soon, every decision, every action, and every initiative was filtered through a people-and-safety-first lens. Employees understood that if they wanted to propose change, they had to honor those two pillars. If it didn't, it simply wasn't ready for leadership review.

And something remarkable happened; leaders began to realize that their legacy wouldn't be defined by metrics alone, but by how they led with empathy, accountability, and a steadfast commitment to people and safety. That's the kind of leadership that endures. That's the kind of culture that transforms.

WHY DO PEOPLE PERISH?

Organizations fail, not because there's no vision written down, but because the vision wasn't translated down to where it matters. When leaders cannot translate the vision successfully, we leave it to our employees to do so on their own. When clear direction is not provided, employees create a multitude of interpretations, and we end up with thousands of viewpoints on the vision. As leaders, we need to continuously share the vision, make it accessible, and understand that the excellent work here never stops.

For many years, I have started meetings, discussions, and even public events describing my vision. Due to the key focus areas for my business, I have been driven by people and safety; therefore, my start and end are always with our people and safety. I have focused on the fundamental components of running a business while placing people and safety first. This has allowed me to create margin, which leads to quality enhancements and more efficient organization.

Companies that can't translate the vision can't possibly translate a legacy to employees. How can employees be passionate about something they can't see? How can employees be driven by a legacy that doesn't exist? They can't! In order to lead with a legacy mindset, we need to clearly translate the fundamental business principles and give our leaders the tools to communicate the basics well.

My greatest accomplishments have not come from the millions of dollars I've brought to the table through increased efficiency without sacrificing safety, executing beyond compliance, or developing high-performing organizations. My biggest accomplishments throughout my career have been uniting teams, painting a vision, setting strategy, and placing people and safety first to achieve our goals. For most successful executives, it's not about position or power but about having our people catch the vision and run with it.

GET TO WORK:

1. Make the vision tangible. Turn your company's vision into three to six clear, relatable focus areas your team can remember and act on.
2. Lead with the vision daily. Start meetings and decisions with the vision in mind, especially people in safety, and stay aligned.
3. Equip leaders to share the "why." Culture leaders should clearly explain the vision and connect it to daily work across all levels.

4
EXAMPLES OF BUILDING A VISION

"Write the vision; make it plain... so that a herald may run with it."
Habakkuk 2:2 NIV / KJV

While it's easy to talk about vision, how do you actually make your company's vision a reality? And what does this look like in different industries? In this chapter, I will share a few stories of people who have taken a vision and built a lasting legacy for their families, businesses, and communities.

Habakkuk 2:2 teaches leaders a profound lesson on vision and communication: *"Write the vision; make it plain... so that a herald may run with it."* In biblical language, a herald was a trusted messenger, one who carried the words of a king with accuracy, urgency, and full understanding. A herald didn't speak for himself; he delivered the message exactly as it was given, able to give an account for its meaning and ready to ensure it reached those who needed to hear it. In the same way, leaders today must craft and communicate a vision that is so clear, so well-defined, and so deeply rooted in purpose that others can carry it forward faithfully. A clear vision transcends time and circumstance, guiding people even when challenges arise. When leaders "make the vision plain," they empower their teams, like heralds, to not only run with the message but to champion it, live it, and ensure the good work it represents is carried out with integrity long after the initial words are spoken.

One element that is common across all of these stories is that the visionary didn't do this work alone. Instead, they got others to buy into the vision and help make it a reality together. Be encouraged by these stories and inspired to take the vision you have and make it accessible for others to join you in achieving it.

FIRST COMES BASICS, THEN COMES EXCELLENCE

One of the most exciting jobs I had was running gas pipeline operations and maintenance within the state of California. My role took me from the Colorado River at the border of California and Arizona to Burney, California, near the Oregon border. I loved the people and the fact that I was able to stretch my skills beyond engineering, finance, and project management.

I was in a new state, with individuals who knew much more than I did about maintaining and operating pipelines. They were rich with knowledge, and there was no denying that my impact on the team would not come from my technical knowledge.

My vision was simple: focus on the basics and remove barriers that kept employees from doing their work well. As I visited underground storage facilities, compressor stations, and regulator stations, I quickly learned that focusing on the basics would allow me to ground the team on what truly mattered: safely moving gas without serious operational events.

Early in my journey, I was working at our San Ramon office when I received a call that my measurement and regulation team had an operational event. I was nearly two hours away and asked the leader to meet me there with the team to discuss what had happened. When I arrived, I found a group of technicians who didn't want to say more for fear of being reprimanded. I could tell that they had collaborated on a story to tell me.

I started by saying, "I'm here to learn, not to find fault. If you all share what happened, we can help teach others and put controls in place so it doesn't happen again. No one is going to get in trouble; I just need the truth so I can help. Teach me."

The team was shocked. I'm not sure if it's because of what I said or the fact that I had driven hours to meet them, but eventually, we were able to have a productive conversation that set the tone for our growth as a team. This discussion laid the groundwork for significant improvements we would see over the next year. The team was honest about why the event occurred and what they needed to keep it from happening again. They also shared how they had previously brought up challenges that had gone unresolved. Over time, this team became champions for the process improvements we would make around causal evaluation, Corrective Action Program, and human performance strategies.

My focus on the basics allowed me to quickly assess many of the challenges within the department and begin enhancing the areas where we needed to be safer, more reliable, and ultimately more efficient. Focusing on the basics created margin, which allowed me to focus on the enhancements and stretch goals. Focus on the basics first, then create a margin for excellence!

BACK TO THE BASICS

In my career, there have been two distinct cases where I've seen a clear vision come to life with repeatable results. In 2010, I saw Pacific Gas and Electric paint a basic, aspirational, and timeless vision after the San Bruno incident. Then, in 2019, I was able to bring the lessons I learned to NiSource and watch the vision take shape after the Merrimack Valley incident. Both visions gave me a unique perspective for helping companies recover and an understanding of how to establish long-lasting cultures of excellence. In both cases, I learned that if the vision can come to life with the basics in mind, employees will gravitate toward achieving the vision with passion and as one team.

After both events, we decided to embark on a Safety Management System journey. Our SMS vision was to focus on the essentials and translate this message in a simple manner that could be carried out by all departments. We used three key foundational pillars to carry our SMS journey forward: safety culture, asset management, and process safety.

Safety culture spoke of a company culture where people would go home safely, the same way they came to work at the start of the day. It meant speaking up and utilizing stop-work authority when an employee saw something wrong. Safety culture challenged us to learn from all events and opportunities.

Asset management addressed all of our asset classes, drove toward risk-informed decision-making, and ensured that we understood how assets were living their lives. Based on our assessments, we drove risk reduction per dollar spent, ensuring that we were reducing the most risk within our gas pipeline assets. This drove the utilization of our CAP and created a culture of finding and resolving issues.

Process safety helped to create a rigorous structure for all employees to show up to work each day and ask the following questions:

- What could go wrong?
- How bad could it be?
- How often could it happen?
- What controls are in place?
- What additional controls are warranted?

It allowed us to look for low-probability, high-consequence events and address these opportunities quickly and effectively.

When carrying a vision for our employees, it's essential to start with the basics. We must determine which components are essential for the organization to run effectively. In the utility space, compliance is essential. For the most part, one can turn the pages of

49 Code of Federal Regulations Part 192 and determine the minimum requirements for compliance. While they aren't flashy or exciting, these essentials are important and need to be our starting point.

These basic components of our businesses must be consistently followed to drive a successful organization. Regardless of the company, there are always items necessary to properly run the business. These requirements are often implemented to reduce risks by identifying the inherent threats and keeping them from maturing into tangible risks. These foundational components are not meant to remove all risks but are a starting point for safe operations. In other words, utilities must start with 49 CFR, followed by an evaluation of their risk profile to understand what additional actions need to be taken.

We can err when we assume that the basics are being followed within our organizations, missing the opportunity to fix essential building blocks of any successful organization. No matter your industry, title, or number of years in the business, you never graduate from the basics.

DENTISTRY THAT MAKES A DIFFERENCE

My in-laws, Ron and Gale Lang, ran a successful dental practice, Marketplace Dental, that they built from scratch nearly forty years ago. They lived on the top floor of the practice, and while Ron would start his day downstairs, Gale took care of their two girls upstairs. Ron's passion for people and his dedication to quality care resonated for years, growing his clientele and building a business that could be trusted by many. The vision was simple, and the tagline read, "Dentistry that makes a difference."

Ron focused on the basics, and these resonated with the people he served. Marketplace Dental became a place that residents of Oak Creek, Wisconsin, could trust. Over the years, Ron built a team that focused on exceeding expectations in quality and service. This simple model focused on the basics of dentistry, producing a successful business that Ron and his family could be proud of.

After nineteen years of marriage to my wife, Hilary, I've spent enough time with Ron to understand that his passion for quality was essential for his grounding in the basics of running his practice. His passion overflows into other areas of life as well; whether it's helping me fix things around the house or his wonderful baking skills, Ron pours his heart into all he does. Those who saw his practice before he retired would have told you that his business was a place that was forward-looking, innovative, and went above and beyond just meeting the minimum requirements of compliance.

Ron figured out how to be brilliant at the basics, and it paid off. His focus and attention to detail in the near term meant less risk to the company and more satisfied customers. In the long term, he was able to build a dynamic and engaged team that wanted to be part of this vision. His practice was innovative, showcasing state-of-the-art dental tools and equipment, and was known for an environment where customers wanted to come back. We tend to create complex visions that sound impressive in executive meetings or when talking to professors, but they don't resonate with those on the front lines.

For Ron, the front line included the dental hygienists and other dentists who joined his vision for Marketplace Dental. He created something straightforward but impactful, attracting people with the idea of "Dentistry that makes a difference." This difference was felt not only by the employees but also by every customer who walked through the door and appreciated the vision he established.

Today, that vision remains a timeless part of the community, all thanks to Ron's focus on people, not just those who worked for him but also the clients he had the privilege of serving for many years.

THE JOURNEY OF A LIFELONG AVIATOR: BOB'S LEGACY OF PASSION AND TEACHING

When I think of visionaries who created a lasting vision, I can think of no finer example than Bob Reynolds. His story is one of dedication, mentorship, and a legacy that goes far beyond just flying planes.

Bob's journey into aviation started long before he ever set foot in an aircraft. His dad, 2nd Lt. James R. Reynolds, a flight instructor during World War II, was deeply involved in the Navy's flight training program and later served in the Air Force. Bob has vivid memories of being taken up to the control tower, watching the planes lined up on the runway, and soaking in every detail about flight. Those early experiences with his father laid the foundation for Bob's lifelong passion.

As Bob grew older, he followed in his father's footsteps and enlisted in the military. He initially trained as an Army helicopter mechanic, but during his service, he switched paths and became a radio operator. That decision kept him away from the dangers of being a flying door gunner on combat helicopters in Vietnam. It was during this time that Bob realized his true passion wasn't helicopters, but fixed-wing aircraft.

After his military service, Bob returned to the States and focused on his education, eventually finding his calling as an educator. When he had the opportunity to start the Catalina High School Aviation Magnet Program, his passion for teaching truly took off.

For years, Bob worked tirelessly to establish a high school aviation program in Tucson, Arizona. Through dedication and perseverance, he earned the trust of parents, government leaders, and school officials, securing millions of dollars in funding. This became the foundation of the Catalina Aerotech program, a place where students could develop technical skills in aviation repair and maintenance and even pursue a fully funded pilot's license if they maintained their grades.

The program grew to over six hundred students, and under Bob's leadership, it became one of the top aviation programs in the country. Bob didn't just teach kids how to fly; he gave them hands-on experience with aircraft, avionics, and even simulated airline ticketing. His work opened students' eyes to the vast potential of aviation and gave them the tools to chase their dreams.

Bob's journey is not just about the planes he's flown or the certificates he's earned. It's about the countless lives he's touched along the way through his students, his work, and the families he helped shape. His legacy is one of giving back, helping others soar just as his father helped him take flight years earlier.

I, too, am a recipient of Bob's legacy.

When I was a first-year high school student, I heard about a program that taught students how to fly. Under his guidance, I began my introductory flights at fourteen years old, and before graduating high school, I had earned my private pilot's license. Aviation has been woven into the fabric of my life, a legacy passed down through generations in my family.

At my father's house, aviation wasn't just admired; it was celebrated. My father often reminisced about flying in his company's plane, a Douglas DC-3. To this day, he considers it one of the best planes ever made because of its reliability, craftsmanship, and sheer joy of flight. Our dinner table became a hub of aviation stories rooted in my grandparents' legacy. My grandfather, on my mother's side, was a Navy pilot during World War II. He married my grandmother, a trailblazer who became one of the first female aviators in Panama. Their passion for aviation carried forward through our family and into my own life.

Aviation became more than a career path—it became part of who I am. Flying is not just my family's past; it is my heritage and the story I proudly carry forward.

Aviation taught me how to navigate the skies, follow VORs across Arizona and California, and manage inevitable mechanical challenges mid-flight. I've lost battery power, encountered inattentive pilots, and flown while terribly sick, knowing I couldn't simply pull over.

One requirement for every private pilot is a long cross-country flight. Mine took me from Avra Valley Airport (now Marana Regional Airport) to Blythe, California.

I remember that day clearly. Everything felt like it was going wrong. I had chosen the airplane everyone wanted to fly, but a mix-up at the flight school resulted in the planes being switched. As I was taking off from Runway 30, another pilot landed without announcing his approach at the uncontrolled field, forcing me into an immediate stop and a second takeoff attempt.

The flight to Blythe was rough, and I became very sick. I relied on breathing, prayer, and focus to manage the discomfort. When I arrived, the winds were terrible, and I couldn't turn back due to fuel limitations. I had to perform a difficult crosswind landing that tested every skill I had learned.

After landing, someone from the FBO ran toward me, waving their hands, telling me I had taken the wrong plane and needed to return immediately. Exhausted, I took a short break before flying back. I was only sixteen years old, entrusted with an enormous responsibility. I remember feeling on cloud nine; I had flown to California, overcome obstacles, and done it with more experience behind an airplane yoke than a car steering wheel.

At the time, I had no idea that the stop-work authority I exercised, the checklists I followed, and the mental rigor I developed would later shape my career in the natural gas industry. A sixteen-year-old could never have known that, but Bob Reynolds did.

Bob gave me the opportunity. The FAA allowed me to complete the flight safely. The mission of Catalina Aero Tech was simple: "A Plan for Success." Those lessons taught me how to manage stress, solve problems, and see beyond immediate obstacles.

Aviation taught me leadership: how to plan, anticipate, and accept that humans make mistakes. Without systems like checklists, failure is likely.

Those lessons surfaced later in my career—during the San Bruno incident, before the commission, and while helping organizations transform their culture. Aviation became an avenue for leadership growth.

Bob never pushed us toward a specific career. He introduced us to pilots, air traffic controllers, and leaders, modeling the qualities he wanted us to adopt. His vision was grounded in building leaders for our communities.

Years later, I called Bob to thank him. Despite the time that had passed, it felt like we were back in the 90s, talking about family, life, and planes. I thanked him, and he reminded me that his vision was never just about flying.

It was about people.

Most pilots rush to earn their license, but we spent four years learning, watching, meeting, and flying. Years later, Bob could still name where my peers ended up: military, mechanics, airline pilots, and even a gas engineer. He remembered us all.

No matter where we landed, we carried his lessons forward.

We are better today because of one man's passion. Aviation was the vehicle, but leadership was the destination. Bob Reynolds painted a vision that continues through us as we lead organizations, families, and communities.

I was fortunate to be part of that vision, and I will always be grateful.

APPLYING THE VISION TO EVERYTHING WE DO

No matter our industry, vision is important. Without that vision, we don't have a common goal to work toward as a team. But it's the leader's responsibility to take that vision and make it accessible to employees. If the vision isn't clear, relevant, and actionable, it will remain a nice idea or a cute catchphrase.

My parents, Tony and Margaret, Ron and Gale, and Bob Reynolds all demonstrated the ability to cast a vision that people wanted to be part of and give them opportunities to get involved and the room to run with it. These incredible leaders and so many more have been able to lead lasting legacies because their vision was clear. And we can do the same with our teams.

Simply put, without vision, people perish. And it's our privilege as leaders to ensure that the vision is clear so that our employees can run with it.

GET TO WORK:

1. How clearly have I translated my vision into basic, actionable steps that others can support and build upon? Am I grounding my team in what matters most?
2. Who have I invited into the process to help carry the vision forward, and have I made it accessible and compelling for them to join?
3. Am I taking time to listen to my employees, understanding if they share the passion for the vision that has been placed in front of them?

5
WHAT'S UNDER THE HOOD

A good name is more desirable than great riches; to be esteemed is better than silver or gold."
Proverbs 22:1 NIV

The last chapter focuses on outward vision; however, we must bridge the gap between *what* a leader communicates and *who* that leader actually is. Who we are as individuals has always been, and will continue to be, more important than any of our accomplishments, degrees, titles, or any other status symbol. As Proverbs 22:1 reminds us, who we are, our name, our character, and our reputation, is worth more than anything we can earn, build, or own. And who you are will reveal itself to your employees and those around you in how you care. Why is it important to consistently reflect on how we are showing up and caring for employees? Simply put, doing so will help us better connect and build trust with our people. Titles, bonuses, stock, and recognition may matter in the moment, but in God's eyes, and in the lives of the people we serve, our character is the legacy.

Every day, we are presented with opportunities to learn more about ourselves and how we show up through our actions. We get to decide how to show our teams that they are the company's most valuable asset. Employees will always see through the leaders who place their priorities, talents, status, or power ahead of their ability to care for those they have the honor of serving.

When who we are becomes more important than anything else, we can better understand our people, their needs, and their passions. For a moment, place your titles aside and focus on what's inside and what may need to change. Engaging in this practice will help us as we grow and gain more responsibility. When we know who we are, we are more ready to lead with a heart and mind on our people.

DRIVING AND LEADING

I drive a variety of Toyota Series 40 and 60 Land Cruisers. These vehicles have accompanied me across the United States and throughout California, Arizona, and Ohio. They are time capsules, machines that have traversed hundreds of thousands of miles and quietly become part of the Mojica family tradition. Land Cruisers have followed me to the field as an engineer; they've been there fishing with my boys, and they've been part of countless late-night ice cream outings where the tailgate became our park bench.

I fell in love with Land Cruisers when I was young. Growing up in Panama, Land Cruisers were the workhorses of farms. The 60 Series (or FJ60, as it's commonly called) was a status symbol; you had made it. This boxy, 1980s-looking whale of a car made you feel safe, capable, and ready for whatever adventure came your way.

Driving an old car, especially an old Land Cruiser, is a magical experience. It's a symphony of mechanical sounds that moves you through life as if nothing is more important than enjoying the ride. It gives you time to think, to explore, to notice the beauty around you. Driving a Land Cruiser makes you forget about time and speed. It reminds you of when life was slower, and people seemed more patient with each other.

So why cars? To me, driving is something magical.

It's the smell of history, the mix of old vinyl, a hint of fuel, warm oil, and a dusty heater that tells you this truck has lived a good life. It's been loved. Like a grandfather everyone wants to listen to, it quietly asks to be heard. And it's more than nostalgia; it's the sound of something mechanical, not digital like today.

I love the straight-six rumble of a Land Cruiser, the slight whine of the gearbox, and the doors that close with a solid thunk. It's not the soft click of modern cars; everything sounds honest. Mechanical. You feel the road, not a computer. The steering has a little play, the suspension actually moves over bumps, and the shifter requires a real hand. Sometimes you have to work it in there. You're not piloting an appliance; you're driving a machine.

Time slows down when I drive with my wife. Maybe people were more patient back then because these cars didn't go that fast. In an old Land Cruiser, you're not rushing; you're moving through the world at the right speed, noticing things you'd blow past in a modern car. There's no CarPlay to distract you. Every drive feels like a small adventure; even a grocery run feels like a trail ride. The high seating position, elevated hood, simple gauges, and quiet confidence make you feel like you could keep going much farther if you wanted.

Family stories are written into the seats. Kids in the back, snacks everywhere, someone leaning forward between the seats to tell a story. The music is low, the laughter is high. Memories get embedded into the fabric and floor mats. It becomes a rolling classroom, teaching your kids how the choke works while you double-clutch, how to listen to the engine, or how to shift without the clutch because you've synchronized those gears perfectly. You're passing down more than car skills; you're passing down curiosity and confidence.

You feel connected to your own past. The truck reminds you of late nights working on it when things didn't always go well. You think of early cars, early roads, maybe time spent with your dad or grandpa, while at the same time building a legacy with your kids. You're never anonymous. People wave. They ask questions at the gas station and share their own Land Cruiser stories. They crawl underneath and wonder how these vehicles you've kept for so long haven't rusted away.

Driving these vehicles feels like being part of a quiet brother-hood, one that appreciates old, honest things. A capability you can touch. Bigger tires, simpler four-by-four levers, metal you can bang your knuckles on. It feels like a tool built to outlast you, and that brings a strange kind of peace.

That's what driving a Land Cruiser is all about.

Land Cruiser is an easily recognized brand. But these cars didn't rise to prominence because of their logo, name, or distinctive style. The Land Cruiser is the car behind the badge; what's under the hood is what makes this vehicle special, ensuring it stands the test of time.

These cars have served as ambulances and diplomatic vehi-cles. Land Cruisers have delivered medical supplies where no other cars could enter and hauled machine guns in war zones. I have a picture of my grandfather and his company-provided Land Cruiser FJ40, a vehicle that was the topic of many discussions, a vehicle we reminisced about for many years. My 1986 Land Cruiser FJ60 has over 270,000 miles and is still running like it could go 500,000 more.

Land Cruisers were built with purpose, with front steering knuckles that could steer a bulldozer and sheet metal that could take a hit, including from the various basketballs and footballs my kids have thrown at it. They were simple, even for their time, almost like a car that refused to step into the future because it always knew where it started and what its purpose was. The Land Cruiser doesn't worry about its name and the status symbol it became for diplomats around the world; it only cares that it can serve its purpose in all it does throughout the world.

As leaders, we carry a badge or a title that can define who we are: doctor, engineer, architect, lawyer, president, VP, SVP, EVP, CIO, CFO, COO, CEO, CHRO, and on and on. These badges may be easily recognizable throughout our fields, but there's no doubt that who you are is more important than your title. What is under the hood is of utmost value.

We are more than badges; we are individuals who have been given special privileges and abilities to care for, build, and support those within our teams. It's always been about our people, and it will never stop being about the people; without them, we are only badges.

So, who are you? Are you focused on the badge that comes with your leadership title?

Or are you focused on what really matters, the character underneath that title?

Leading a legacy means leading our people in such a way that our legacy will live on; it's choosing to shape the future, not just being remembered by it. After all, legacy is about making a difference that will endure long after we're gone. Few people will positively remember the leader who didn't care about or who considered themselves more important than the people they were there to serve.

For me, each day counts more and more as I've realized that I'm building new executives to take my place, those who will make their voices and actions heard to make a positive difference in this world. I'm not as concerned about their badges; I'm interested in who they are as human beings. Will they lead with a purpose? Will they pass the legacy forward?

I'm confronted with these questions more often today than when I was a young frontline leader. Back then, it was hard to think about legacy, as my leaders were pushing for MBAs, corporate training, executive preparation programs, special projects, and even the occasional temporary assignments to signal to upper management that I was a candidate for advancement. All these things are important, but none of these programs prepare the leader for what matters most: how to serve those we lead.

Two key pillars that have helped me throughout my career are creating a culture centered on connection and trust.

CONNECTION

Creating a legacy doesn't happen overnight. It takes time and continuous engagement to foster connections that will last. There are a wide variety of ways to connect with our employees, and I would encourage all of us to continually evaluate our performance.

When my family and I left Panama to come to the United States, we made sure to remember our traditions and where we came from. My father brought his collection of cassette tapes from local artists that we often played as we drove around Tucson, Arizona. We also maintained our love for boxing, which was to us what football is to the United States.

My family's ties to boxing ran deep; my grandfather had wrapped the hands of the great Panamanian boxer Roberto Duran. Duran had even dedicated a couple of fights to my grandmother for her support of the people of Santiago,

Panama. As the dictatorship of Manuel Noriega grew, Duran became the glue that held the Panamanian people together. Duran, known to the world as *"Manos de Piedra,"* or "Hands of Stone," was feared in the ring. His punches carried a power that could end a fight in an instant, and his opponents knew it. But he didn't just rely on strength; he moved with a strategy and intensity that made him nearly unstoppable. He conquered the ring with skill, heart, and an unshakable will, becoming a legend not just in boxing but also for the people of Panama.

His prominent boxing career, filled with ups and downs, helped Panamanians share his wins as a win for the country. Duran had witnessed the power that had been held by Noriega's tyrannical government for years, but he had learned something far more important. While Noriega infused fear in Panamanians, Duran's passion for the people of Panama ran deeper and held exponentially more weight than any dictator could wield. In the 2019 documentary titled *I Am Duran*, Duran stated, "Noriega had the power... I had the people."

This sentiment is also true for us as leaders. Repeatedly, I've heard employees say things like, "I don't have the title," or "People won't listen unless it comes from above." Individuals often perceive that it's essential to have a certain position or title to drive decisions with an appropriate level of power. But that's simply not the case.

In reality, we can all start leading without a title. Everyone can lead from where they are. We can lead from any seat we fill by getting out there and caring for people. As a young engineer, I was energized by supporting the field; I was constantly looking for ways to help the team. They had much more experience than I, and asking them questions while offering my assistance opened a door for improved collaboration across our teams. I had virtually no power; I had no "badge." I only had a willingness to help and show them that I cared.

Titles will only get you so far. Like Duran, if you have the people, you have the company. I focused on caring for the people, and by the time I got the badge, it served as an opportunity to do more for those who had been with me all the way. The truth is that when you care for people, they will care for you. Remember, you will spend more time at work with people who aren't your family than with those you are close to at home; don't miss the opportunity to win their hearts and minds with your engagement.

Connecting with our employees can come in so many ways. I've found that one of the most impactful ways to connect is to understand what employees do each and every day. Our employees are often eager to tell us what needs to change. When their feedback is received and adequately dealt with, we connect with their work, build trust, and begin creating a culture of continuous improvement.

Trust

Trust takes years to build, and after it's earned, it can take seconds to deteriorate. How you show up over time builds this trust, and leaders don't get a pass on the rules of engagement.

Early in my career, I made a personal commitment that I would never allow my actions to break trust. From an early age, I understood how important trust is, how fragile it is, and how easily it can be lost. I have also learned that people are always watching, providing opportunities for trust to be built or for trust to disintegrate.

A few years ago, I traveled with a fellow leader to a site to meet with employees and recognize one of my team members for his excellent work. When we arrived at the equipment yard, we didn't realize that employees were already waiting outside and filming our entrance. Though we didn't know it at the time, the way we pulled into the parking lot was an opportunity to build trust with the team.

Our company policy was clear: vehicles needed to be backed into parking spaces when possible. If there was a passenger, they needed to serve as a spotter, helping the driver to back the vehicle into the parking space. This simple policy enhanced safety during parking and helped facilitate a positive safety culture; there was no question that it needed to be followed.

When we arrived on site, we followed the policy. I stepped out of the vehicle to help the leader back the vehicle into the parking space. Then we walked into the building, celebrated the recognition, and headed back to the corporate office.

Weeks later, a separate leader pulled me aside and showed me the video of us following policy and backing the vehicle in. When we followed the rules, they were impressed, and it built trust. It also helped that leader in his efforts to drive safety at his level.

The truth is that employees are always watching how leadership behaves. We don't get a pass when it comes to how we show up. Trust is built through consistency in keeping our promises; every decision, whether big or small, is an opportunity for trust to develop.

Trust is built an inch at a time and lost a mile at a time. This is why it's so important to focus on trust. Even if we have the trust of our employees, we must continue to build on that foundation. When we grow stagnant or complacent, we may begin to lose that trust. Our teams and organizations need consistent care and support. We must constantly observe our behaviors and ask ourselves if we are slipping.

Years ago, I was introduced to a simple tool that I utilize each month. I have a list of the names of my family members, direct reports, peers, and key stakeholders, including skip-level leaders across my organization; I place a checkmark by each name of individuals I connect with, and it has become a powerful reflection for me. At the end of the week, I review the list, quickly assess where I'm not spending enough time, and make adjustments the following week to address those opportunities.

It may sound silly, but nurturing these relationships is important and requires intentionality. I have found that we can perceive that we have stronger relationships than we really have; it's not until we assess ourselves and the time we spend building trust that we realize areas of improvement. Trust is so important that no relationship can afford to be overlooked.

LEAD WHERE YOU ARE

Leadership is not conferred by a title, badge, or corner office. It is earned through character, consistency, and impact. Every person leads through influence, choices, relationships, and example, regardless of role or position.

Several years ago, my parents and my wife surprised me by having my degree placed on the official University of Arizona placard that now hangs over my desk. Each morning, as I walk into my office, I see Old Main, the university's first building, dating back to 1891, above my diploma. It reminds me of the work, sacrifice, and perseverance it took to earn that degree. But it also reminds me of something more important: that credential is not what defines me as a leader. Titles may grant authority, but they do not create leadership. What's under the hood always matters more than what's on the door.

If you've been entrusted with a title, a badge, or positional authority, use it, not to elevate yourself but to serve others. Leadership is stewardship. A title doesn't give you permission to lead; it gives you greater responsibility to protect, develop, and advocate for those in your care. It simply expands your platform; it does not replace your obligation to lead with humility, integrity, and courage.

And if you don't yet have the title, you are not disqualified; you are being trained. Some of the most meaningful leadership moments of my career happened long before I had positional authority. I learned that listening, truly listening, opened doors no title ever could. By hearing concerns at the ground level, removing obstacles, and responding with action, trust began to form. That trust became influence. Influence became opportunity. Those same listening skills that helped me lead without authority became my greatest strength when authority was eventually entrusted to me.

Leadership grows in proximity in hallway conversations, job sites, break rooms, and water-cooler moments where real issues surface and real trust is built. Fixing small problems others overlook often creates the credibility that earns you the chance to solve bigger ones. This is how hearts and minds are won, not through position but through presence.

Lead from the chair you've been given. Lead with excellence where your feet are planted. Build trust deliberately. Serve consistently. Grow intentionally. When you do, your leadership will not go unnoticed, not because you sought recognition but because your impact became undeniable.

Don't chase badges. Don't wait for titles. Don't postpone leadership.

Focus on what's under the hood and lead right where you are.

Oh, and before I forget… drive a Land Cruiser before you die. Trust me on that one.

GET TO WORK:

1. Check your character. Write down three words your team would use to describe you. Then pick one

behavior you'll adjust this week to better reflect who you truly are under the hood.

2. Build visible trust. Choose one concrete action to practice consistently over the month. This could be transparently communicating the rationale behind major decisions, following through on commitments to key stakeholders, or proactively collaborating with other executives to align on company priorities. Make your actions visible, and at the end of the month, ask your team and peers for feedback: What did they notice? Where did your consistency make an impact?
3. Connect with intention: List five people you lead or influence. Reach out to one each day; listen, ask how they're doing, and find one way to help remove a barrier for them.

6
WHAT DOES GOOD LOOK LIKE?

"Let us not become weary in doing good, for at the proper time we will reap a harvest if we do not give up."
Galatians 6:9 NIV

C haracter alone doesn't provide a roadmap; it provides the integrity to follow one. By defining a clear standard of "good," a leader with character can translate their internal values into external, repeatable excellence.

The question, "What does good look like?" has become a foundational piece of my leadership philosophy, and I have met so many great leaders who say the same. This question sparks the attention of leaders who aim to constantly improve, generating ideas that invigorate our meeting rooms with provocative thoughts about how we can be better.

At its core, this question reflects a deeper truth echoed in Galatians 6:9: "Let us not become weary in doing good." It reminds us that doing good is not a one-time act but a daily discipline, one that should reach into every part of our lives, at home, at work, and especially in how we treat the people around us. That truth has shaped how I think about leadership and why I continue to ask what good looks like in every role I take on.

"What does good look like?" is more than a question; it's a process I learned over time. Today, it's impossible for me to approach any role without a thorough look into where my team is and where we need to go. This question challenges us to listen to our employees, protect them, and invest in them so they can thrive, while also ensuring we take care of our companies through integrity, safety, and long-term stewardship.

This question has taken me across industries: aviation, gas and electric utilities, nuclear, medicine, waste management, telecommunications, manufacturing, and more, to learn how to best attain and define what good looks like. Learning what good looks like in one company has led me to establish the foundation for good in others, constantly reshaping my view of good as processes and strategies have improved over time. Once I experienced good, the bar continued to rise, which is the type of continuous improvement we all want at our companies.

The knowledge I gained from my time as an engineer replacing service and main pipelines in Tucson, Arizona, became pivotal in the work I would help my teams accomplish many years later. Those early lessons were essential in helping me define the challenges we faced, the opportunities for improvement, and the roadmap I would lay out for how to improve the way companies operate. These learnings have shaped my understanding of the problems that frontline employees face while also giving me a unique perspective on what needs to be done to optimize the company's performance based on inefficiencies and opportunities.

Early in my career, "good" meant paper or microfiche maps used to identify the approximate locations of underground utilities stretching throughout the United States. Maps are utilized to paint a three-dimensional view of the underground infrastructure, allowing companies to reroute new pipelines, repair leaks, replace existing pipelines, and even determine if new public improvement projects will be in conflict with existing infrastructure. The paper maps were difficult to view from the field, but they were the best the industry had at that point.

The definition of "good" changed when laptops became widely available, giving field employees and engineers more accurate data that was updated more frequently. As technology changed, so did our definition of good. And our definition only continues to evolve. Now, utility employees use tablets that have seemingly endless mapping information, some of which includes geospatial information on assets relative to municipal infrastructure and other utilities. This is information that is used for probabilistic risk assessments, coupled with maintenance history, and even the integration of neural networks that use AI to make better business decisions.

Today, the amount of data we can gather from our maps is paramount in helping us make decisions about threats to assets, understand aging infrastructure, and route our vehicles to serve customer needs. Our definition of good today is driving more timely decision-making processes for how to operate a gas utility. This has come from years and years of asking what good looks like and iterating on that question to paint a roadmap for the future.

Early in my career, asking, "What does good look like?" helped me understand what was needed for employees in and out of the field. Over twenty-five years later, that same question has led me to help design and implement industry-leading tools and processes that are revolutionizing the way we look at our business. I'm confident that in years to come, the industry will continue to lift itself above where we are today and achieve even better outcomes than what we can currently imagine.

Without this question, it is difficult to set benchmarks, and it's almost impossible for employees to understand the steps needed to achieve these goals.

Focusing on identifying, developing, and delivering *good* has been pivotal to every company I have been at. And I believe that the same is true for you. No matter your industry, title, or responsibilities, asking "What does good look like?" and committing to not grow weary in doing good can revolutionize your company.

In the following pages, we will examine what good is, why it is important, and how driving good leads to lasting changes in employees and organizations.

WHAT IS GOOD?

Today, as I lead new teams, I intentionally listen to employees to learn where their hearts and minds are to then help pave the road (the vision) for where we are going. What good looks like empowers us to find the appropriate strategies, help employees feel proud of the work they do, and be energized to permeate that vision across the organization. When our employees can grasp this concept, they set aggressive goals that spark them to think freely and ultimately align their passions with the needs of the company.

This is often referred to as the line-of-sight mentality. In other words, can we help employees see the beginning and the end through the goals we create? Think of a bow and arrow. If you fire your arrow at a target, but there's something blocking the way, your arrow might not arrive at its final destination. However, if you take the time to move the obstruction, the arrow will cut through the air without resistance and easily find its way to the goal; in other words, the arrow will have a line of sight to get from A to B.

When we focus on defining what good is, we set the tone for the organization. A line-of-sight mentality provides outstanding clarity about what it means to be good at the work we perform. These goals help employees know what a good day looks like and empower them to utilize the appropriate metrics to drive the desired results.

So, what is good? Good is knowing what it takes to drive our companies to excellence. It means clearly understanding our starting point and creating a vision and strategy for all employees to get there. The fundamental question of what good looks like must be foundational for every leader embarking on new projects, developing innovative strategies, leading top-performing organizations, and driving continuous improvement.

Good means creating strategies we can be proud of. Good is about creating a line of sight for our employees from start to finish. Good is about driving excellence within our companies through solid benchmarking strategies.

It's our responsibility as leaders to understand that we must start with good and never stop looking for good in our teams, companies, and industries.

GOOD COMING TO LIFE

One of my favorite encounters with this process came under the leadership of Jesus J. Soto, who led the Gas Operations department within PG&E after the San Bruno, California incident. We worked together for over five years, and during that time, I watched him model the behaviors that helped shape the strategic vision for our teams while also driving practices that have been reproduced throughout the industry.

I witnessed good come to life under Jesus' leadership. His philosophy was simple and effective: "How can you know where you're going if you don't know where to start?" Through Jesus' leadership at PG&E, we were able to drive safety across a variety of pipeline safety measures, often going above top industry benchmarks and surpassing industry performance in many key areas. For the most part, gas utilities follow a remarkably similar playbook for success: safe, reliable, and affordable delivery of natural gas throughout the communities we serve.

After the San Bruno incident, the stakes were higher for us than for any other utility in the United States. In our eyes, the entire country was watching our response, and the pressure was high. The leadership team rallied together to ensure that, as Jesus would later say, "Our DO/SAY ratio" equaled one. This meant that if we committed to doing something, we would do it without looking back, and that we would be held accountable for our commitments. This sounds great, but it can be challenging to put into practice. Anyone can commit to small goals, but few commit to goals that stretch our imagination and human will to do better.

We were passionate about driving safety, quality, and reliability, realizing that the journey toward efficiency would catch up to us at some point. In other words, we recognized that our focus needed to be on driving safety, reliability, and affordability. After San Bruno, our primary mission was to start from the ground up, doing all we could to prevent an incident like this from happening again. This process required all of us to stretch different muscles. We challenged each other to ask, "What does good look like?" across the industry. Jesus put it this way: "Asking what good looks like means understanding that someone has already been there, giving individuals an opportunity to drive toward that goal."

I can honestly say that the best two days for leaders seeking to answer the question "What does good look like?" are the day one figures out what good looks like and the day one achieves it—everything in between is hard work. Not to say there's no joy in the journey, but rather a recognition that there is great satisfaction in finally understanding your problem and solving it. Although there's joy in the process, driving "good" is not for the faint of heart.

Jesus led us through this demanding work as we sought to identify the good in our company and industry. As we discussed safety, reliability, and affordability metrics, Jesus prompted questions about our performance, the best performers in the industry, and the gap between us and them. He constantly challenged us to identify the good and be dissatisfied with anything less.

We then asked the same questions within our teams, constantly looking for a better way to deliver on our promises. The culture of looking for good permeated our company like an unstoppable force. We invigorated our teams, and that energy stretched out to the industry. The news was so good it had to be shared. After all, how does a company suffer hardship, learn from those mistakes, and not feel compelled to go back out and share what they've learned with others?

Soon, other companies were coming to us to learn more about our progress, and we were making a difference that lifted the entire industry bench. It was truly an example of rising tides lifting all boats. We were proud of the work our employees were doing and humbled by what we were learning, so we opened our company to allow anyone willing to come, learn, and share.

"Good" became our benchmark to gauge how much time and effort needed to be placed on the task at hand to achieve our vision. *Good* became common nomenclature throughout the halls of our San Ramon, California, office, with leaders and individuals contributing to a process of continuous improvement that taught us all about benchmarking with other companies.

This process taught me to look outside my own industry and learn from others who were doing safety, reliability, and affordability better than we were. My journey took me to the highly secured walls of the Diablo Canyon Nuclear Facility, the Seattle corporate hub of Alaska Airlines, manufacturing companies modeling top industry behaviors, and other domestic and international utilities and companies that had been on similar journeys to success.

It is amazing what can be learned from these conversations across industries. Although the name on the front of the building is different and our companies provide a variety of services, we face the same familiar challenges around people, safety, quality, compliance, and financial stewardship. As mentioned before, these five key areas would drive the foundation for my own journey to help companies succeed—my Five Keys to Success.

GOOD DRIVES YOUR STARTING POINT, BUT CERTAINLY NOT THE END

When companies create audacious goals to reshape the landscape, they must understand who's in front. Gaining this insight paints the roadmap for where to go and the vision for how to excel beyond the walls of conventional thinking.

This is exactly what we did. We started by seeing where others were in order to understand that we could do better if we set our eyes on it. At that time, we had set our vision on a variety of concepts, processes, and strategies that most companies had not even dreamed of embarking on.

One example of this was advanced leak survey technology, which we felt would revolutionize the way gas utilities identify and repair leaks. Utility companies use leak surveys to survey their pipelines at a variety of different time intervals, which split the network of pipelines into sections, allowing leak survey personnel to carefully walk streets and identify the potential for gas pipeline leaks. The process was cumbersome and limited by practices that had matured slowly over many decades. At the time, leak surveyors would walk neighborhood streets with a printed map depicting the approximate location of underground pipelines, marking the paper map to indicate the area that was covered. This process was riddled with opportunities for improvement.

Few were willing to invest in these strategies at that time, despite the proven effectiveness of the new technology. Companies were worried about the number of leaks they would find, how they would repair leaks quickly, and how to approach changes in philosophy with regulatory commissions. Despite the reticence of others, we pressed forward, recognizing that those doing it best within the industry could not come close to the processes we were about to deploy. We were confident we were about to reshape leak survey technology within the industry.

Once we achieved *good*, we had to have a vision for what else could be done. We understood that conventional processes contained a human factor that is not easily addressed with even the best training, processes, or expertise. The only way the problems could be addressed would be through innovative thinking!

We introduced advanced leak survey technology, utilizing cavity ring-down spectroscopy, a fancy name for a tool that would now be one thousand times more sensitive than conventional leak survey equipment. The tool could assess the amount of molecules in the air through careful measuring of the molecular absorption of laser light within the instrument's cavity. Because this tool could now sense leaks much further from the source than conventional equipment, we could be more proactive in identifying and repairing leaks.

The concept led to innovative ways to perform leak surveys, and today, this technology continues to evolve beyond what we could have dreamed of. Yes, we found more leaks, but more importantly, we reduced human error, planned our work better, and understood the size and volume of leaks. Most importantly, this data allowed us to drive down potential safety-related conditions and decrease methane emissions throughout California.

Starting with good led us to a place where we could lead the industry. Almost ten years later, the tools we pioneered are slowly becoming the new "good," challenging companies to perform leak surveys in different ways. The reality is that we would've been far from the best if we just followed the rest of the industry. That's what searching for good does: it helps you understand how good you can be today and gives you the ability to dream of how much better you can be tomorrow.

DRIVING "GOOD"

Any leader who has reached even marginal success knows the challenges that come with achieving difficult goals. More importantly, they understand the Herculean effort that comes from making success repeatable throughout their leadership teams and organizations. I have never been a fan of efforts that are not reproducible and end up being forgotten over time.

Leaders who are passionate about their work devote extensive time and care, making sure that they plant in places where the harvest will be plentiful. They take time to build long-lasting processes that stretch throughout time. These are the leaders who train "good" and coach their teams to challenge themselves. Driving good and creating a culture that values good is how we can lead a legacy. When we set sustainable practices, we lead a legacy that others can build from, a legacy that can be remembered and propels companies to continue to get better and better over time.

I find that many companies often have temporary success with respect to advancing innovative practices. When leadership changes occur, new leaders rarely have a playbook for where to start their own journey of continuous improvement. So, they start over, losing track of what prior leaders tried and improved; they miss the history of the company, failing to recognize the shortfalls and successes of the past. They pull from their own bag of tools that they've used for years instead of talking to employees about what the company has already tried.

We had reached "good," and we had taken time to document our leak survey practices and procedures, allowing future teams and the industry to continue to build from where we had left. We spent considerable time teaching the organization how to look for good, creating a culture that, even years later, still resonates through the employees who continue to drive continuous improvement.

We start by teaching our employees to fail and learn. We must give our employees the ability to try new things and experience wins and losses. As I've trained this muscle, I have found my employees going to companies and returning to our corporate office, excited to try what they just learned. On various occasions, we tried something, only to understand that the formula for success didn't transfer directly within our walls. Each effort we brought back led to more thinking, more talking, and more collaboration, which ultimately resulted in better ways to run our business. I have allowed my teams to dream, succeed, fail, and recover, learning along the way that the process of continuous improvement isn't linear or perfect.

Continuous improvement is about trying, failing, learning, and calibrating our experiences to find the optimal solutions for our business. This concept is often referred to as PDCA, or Plan, Do, Check, and Adjust; we Plan our strategies, Do them,

Check for desired results, and Adjust our strategies as a result.

Today, as I continue to embark on benchmarks, I'm not so interested in just bringing back certain processes, tools, or technologies; my interest is in sparking thoughts that can light up the minds of my leaders. Sometimes, the simple act of watching other companies innovate and being excited about progress brings my leaders back to the office with a renewed sense of passion, gratitude for the work we have the opportunity to perform, and a mindset that drives out-of-the-box thinking.

I teach my staff to look beyond the conventional walls of benchmarking and even outside our industry, because good doesn't live in one place. It shows up everywhere if we train ourselves to see it.

I see good in a Formula One race, where drivers navigate highly engineered machines through tight turns and long straightaways, relying on preparation, trust, and split-second decisions. I see good in my sons as they play soccer, baseball, and basketball, learning teamwork, discipline, and resilience one practice at a time. I see good at church as my pastor walks us through life's challenges with wisdom and grace, and in the way my parents' marriage continues to bloom after so many years, reminding me that commitment and care compound over time.

I notice good at my home airport as pilots take off and land, following precise routines that protect lives most passengers never think twice about. I see it at Lake Michigan, learning from others who have navigated its treacherous currents and storms for decades and still respect its power. Good is present in the quiet, steady way my wife tends our family farm, supports our local 4H chapter, and pours her heart into our boys and me every single day.

The more I look for it, the more I find it. And when I see good come to life, I make a point to call it out and praise it, because recognition reinforces behavior.

I remember the first time I truly saw good modeled in the field by one of my leaders. It wasn't during a meeting or a formal safety briefing. It was in the small things, the moments when most people weren't watching. I noticed him turning shovels over so no one would step on the blades. He taught me to drive through worksites at night to make sure Type II lighted barricades were on and visible. Simple actions, done consistently, that quietly set the tone.

That behavior showed everyone around him what good looked like in practice. And once others saw it modeled, they began to do the same. That's how culture forms. Not through grand speeches, but through everyday actions that speak louder than words.

Good starts with the simple things, but it doesn't end there. Looking for good eventually becomes a way of life. Once we can train in this within our organizations, we can be assured that we will leave a lasting change for those who will take our place in the future.

Driving *good* begins by modeling the appropriate behaviors and then allowing our leaders to practice the same. Continuous improvement doesn't happen overnight; it is about allowing failures to happen and giving others the opportunity to learn and continue to try what will work. This straightforward process allows employees to remove the barriers most of them have around failure.

The truth is that no one wants to fail. But when we allow our employees to practice failure, they rise to the challenge, knowing that through a variety of failures, they will figure out the winning strategy. One win leads to another, and the strategy is energizing as we see employees rise to the occasion by challenging each other through this same thought process. *Give them room to learn, and they will learn, but give them room to fail, and they will deliver on what you never imagined.*

Over the years, I was given plenty of opportunities to fail and learn while exploring better ways to perform the work. Sometimes this led to outstanding results, while other attempts were quickly abandoned based on their limited performance. I have tried and explored so many avenues with my teams. Some have led to remarkable opportunities that have improved performance and user experience and helped drive better-informed decisions; others haven't realized the results we were expecting. But throughout all of these learnings, I have been able to witness my teams achieve industry-leading performance, driving innovative technologies that have set the mark for what good looks like and setting us apart as premier industry players within the market. We have driven *good* together, leading a legacy within both the company culture and the utility industry as a whole.

WHY GOOD, NOT GREAT?

I once asked Jesus why he aimed for "good" instead of "great." He confirmed what I had gathered over many years of working together: he used the words interchangeably.

The reality is that the process of good ultimately and naturally leads to excellence beyond our dreams. Good gives us the opportunity to dream and understand what it takes to be the best. Jesus always knew this, and as he asked the question, his heart was set on being the best.

He shared something else with me that I will never forget: "Good is sometimes good enough." This is a vital component of the process we can't lose track of. In some cases, we realized that once we had achieved good, the value of going beyond good in a specific area wasn't worth the time and energy. Instead, we would turn our attention to something else that was underperforming and needed to become good.

No company is good at everything. The price to pay for perfection in all areas is one that leads to lofty expectations and an overwhelmed staff; it's a price tag that no one can afford. Great companies comprehend this and place value in understanding where to invest the next available dollar to mitigate the highest risks, maximizing each dollar spent.

DRIVING THE GOOD WILL ALWAYS DRIVE EXCELLENCE

Our mission as leaders should be to show our employees how to seek out what "good" looks like each day, eventually driving them to excellence through a relentless approach to continuous improvement. We can start by asking questions:

- What does a good day look like for your department?
- What's a good week for you?
- How about a good month?

Successful leaders know that by winning the day, we win the week, and by winning the week, we win the month. Like any successful sports team, if we win most of those months, we win the year. After all, what good employee or leader doesn't want to win?

Asking our teams to understand what good looks like drives a culture that seeks to better understand what is going well and what isn't. From that place, we can develop strategies to look deep within our organization to continuously recalibrate our strategies for success.

I have witnessed my leaders take on this challenge every day and exceed goals and expectations. These same leaders have experienced greater satisfaction in their jobs, risen to new challenges with an optimistic mindset, and had a more engaged workforce. This is all because they understood the challenges and what it took to be successful and were able to paint an unclouded vision for their teams.

Let's make it real for our teams every day by asking them, "What does *good* look like?"

GET TO WORK:

1. Can I point to a real example of what good looks like in action within my own team right now?
2. Are my people clear on what "good" means, or are they filling in the blanks themselves?
3. How am I benchmarking with other companies throughout the year, what are we learning, and how are we implementing meaningful changes?

7

SAFETY MATTERS
EVERYWHERE

*"The prudent see danger and take refuge, but the simple keep going
and pay the penalty."*
Proverbs 27:12 NIV

Have you ever considered the steps pioneers had to take to make history? We can marvel at Amelia Earhart's first trip across the Atlantic, or the manufacturing of the Model T and its impact on automotive history, or the first flight to space, but how often do we consider the months and years of preparation those feats required? When I think about remarkable events, I like to focus on the safety preparations that were required for the initial idea to become a reality. Proverbs 27:12 reminds us, "The prudent see danger and take refuge, but the simple keep going and pay the penalty." Wisdom does not ignore risk; it recognizes danger and takes action to protect people. That principle sits at the heart of safety, whether at work, at home, on the road, or in our communities.

In 2012, Felix Baumgartner broke skydiving records by jumping from the edge of the stratosphere, utilizing a helium balloon that stretched the height of a fifty-five-story building. Felix would break several world records at the time, including the fastest free-fall speed, longest free-fall, highest manned balloon flight, and highest skydive ever recorded. I remember staring in awe at the television as he made that twenty-four-mile jump from space in his pressurized suit.

Accomplishing this incredible and dangerous feat required Felix and his team to practice again and again, mitigating as much risk as possible. My friend John, an industry expert in aviation safety, described it as an "error-intolerant" event that left no room for mistakes. At nearly the thirty-five-second mark, Felix broke the speed of sound as he traveled back toward Earth. As he began to spiral, he relied on his training, experience, and knowledge to recover from the spin and make it safely to the ground. And he did, proving that this seemingly impossible feat could be done.

The training for the launch required nearly five years of preparation and careful consideration of everything that could go wrong. In a true life-and-death situation, their relentless focus on safety ensured that Felix survived and lived to jump another day. They did not rush past hazards or dismiss procedures; they slowed down, identified the danger, and did the hard work required to protect human life.

And yet, as I was authoring this book, we received the unfortunate news that Felix passed away following a tragic paragliding accident in Italy. This loss is heartbreaking, and my thoughts remain with his family and loved ones. It is important to say this with care: Felix's earlier achievements were the result of extraordinary safety discipline, but his passing serves as a sobering reminder that safety is never something we complete or outgrow.

Even someone who successfully accomplished one of the most challenging and dangerous jumps in history can still be vulnerable to accidents later in life. Investigators later determined that the paragliding accident resulted from human error rather than a mechanical failure, reinforcing a difficult but necessary truth: safety does not happen by chance, and it cannot be relaxed simply because we have succeeded before.

If we truly care about people, safety must be more than a slogan. In my own career, I have tried to make safety a cornerstone of every decision, because putting people first means seeing danger and taking refuge, even when it slows us down. In the utility world, that means ensuring our crews, contractors, and customers go home safe, able to hug their families, sit at their dinner tables, and see tomorrow. Safety is one of the most practical ways we love our neighbor and one of the clearest ways we lead a legacy that honors those entrusted to our care.

This is why maintaining a constant focus on safety is so critical.

But what *is* safety? To answer this question, we must first examine where and why safety matters, and then we will be able to dissect what safety means.

WHERE DOES SAFETY MATTER?

Simply put, safety matters everywhere.

We don't think twice about safety when we take our kids to the doctor or when we take a flight; we expect safety to be a top priority. We expect doctors, pilots, electricians, dentists, construction workers, restaurant servers, first responders, utility workers, and more to provide a standard of care that places safety first. What about others whose professions don't have a clear connection to safety? What about an accountant, teacher, lawyer, bus driver, engineer, or IT professional? Years ago, I probably would have struggled to make the connection myself, but as my career has progressed, I've learned that safety is an essential part of all of our lives.

It's crucial to recognize that social expectations for safety have shifted drastically over time. Today, the minimum expectations for safety have extended beyond error-intolerant industries and migrated into every area of business. Financial decisions can no longer be made in a silo, nor can a teacher take for granted whether students will be safe in a classroom. Safety expectations have increased, a trend that we will surely continue to see. We are bombarded with the use of AI, and we can be certain that the topic of safety will inundate AI discussions and its maturity.

In Panama, my father drove a single-cab Toyota Hilux pickup, a three-passenger vehicle for our family of five. As a child, some of my fondest memories were riding in the back of my father's pickup truck as we traveled through the countryside of Panama. The wind would whip through my hair, carrying with it the scents of fresh rain, the jungle, earthy soil, and distant flowers and trees, as if nature itself was speaking to me. There was a wild, uncontainable freedom in those moments, a feeling that nothing else in the world mattered except the open road, the endless sky, and the rhythm of the tires as we drove.

My father even installed a camper with a wired telephone that allowed us to communicate during longer trips. The bed of the truck became my own little kingdom. It was a space where I could look at the landscape, soaking in every detail of the rolling hills, the clusters of trees, and the scattered homes that dotted the horizon.

That was the standard of care back then: no seat belts, just the freedom of the pickup bed all to myself. Safety standards back in the 80s were vastly different from those of today. Panama had no government mandates for seat belts, and car manufacturers didn't feel compelled to install them.

Fortunately, safety standards have evolved over time. The government created new safety requirements for vehicles, requiring automakers to install seat belts in all designs. The standard of care has also increased, leading car manufacturers to include additional safety measures in their vehicles, and I'm certain this trend will continue with the evolution of autonomous driving.

Across all industries, there is a standard of care woven throughout our culture. For a teacher, it's in how children are taught and cared for. For the IT professional, it's in keeping with rigorous standards of confidentiality and cybersecurity, and for the accountant, it's in detailed and thorough record-keeping.

When decisions are made without the standard of care in mind, they can have detrimental impacts on our people. Safety matters everywhere, no matter our profession, but *why* should we place an emphasis on maintaining a high standard of care across industries?

WHY DOES SAFETY MATTER?

Without safety, we simply cannot run a business we can be proud of. An emphasis on safety must extend beyond personnel or occupational safety to process safety or public safety. All of these components are essential. In his book titled *Energy-Based Safety*, Matt Hollowell states, "For decades, safety was narrowly viewed as the absence of injuries, with a work period considered safe if no one was hurt and unsafe if an injury occurred. This view of safety is reflected in injury rates, zero-injury goals, and signs reporting time since last injury. A hyperfocus on these outcomes has led to an environment where injuries are hidden, and learning is stifled."

Most companies have assets they regard as intrinsic to their business models, and utilities are no different. On the natural gas transportation side of the utility business, there's an intricate network of pipelines that span below and above the ground, traversing roads, highways, valleys, and even mountains to safely deliver natural gas to homes and businesses across the nation. These assets also represent compressor stations, liquefied natural gas facilities, and underground storage fields, which help store gas to be utilized during winter months, and a multitude of regulator stations and valves to control and regulate the flow of gas.

Think about your company. What assets do you value? If those assets fail, or if your processes fail, will your customers, employees, or the public remain safe?

Safety matters everywhere, and when we lose track of this, everything else falls apart. However, when we place an emphasis on safety, we can build an environment where businesses can grow for generations to come.

Safety is the cornerstone of any successful business. When safety is not prioritized, the consequences can be devastating, not just for the individuals involved but for the organization as a whole. A lapse in safety creates an environment of uncertainty and mistrust, leading to decreased morale, higher turnover rates, and potential financial losses. It often takes years and sometimes decades for companies to fully recover from tragic events. No company can thrive in an atmosphere where employees, customers, and stakeholders feel their well-being is secondary to profits or efficiency. Neglecting safety compromises the very foundation upon which a business operates, eventually causing even the most powerful companies to falter.

On the electric side of the utility industry, there are similar components that help move electrons instead of gas molecules, assets such as generation facilities, substations, distribution and transmission lines, and more. These are discussed each day within utility companies, spending significant time addressing asset risk management issues, often in an expedited manner. This is essential in most companies that are asset-intensive.

Leaders who grow up within these asset-intensive environments learn to finely tune assets for optimal performance. Like a perfectly tuned F1 race car, they look for ways to extract the most energy from the company's assets to provide customers with safe, reliable, and affordable services. These leaders look for creative ways to drive innovation, search for better ways to address issues, and are keen on asking appropriate questions to understand what decisions to make.

As a junior engineer, I learned to walk myself through this process of assessing asset-related conditions and work to resolve issues quickly and effectively. In some of the most innovative utility companies, there's a place where companies can typically see everything that is happening across their service territory: the Daily Morning Call. This allows us to quickly see which generation units are operating, how outages are progressing, and understand load demands on the system. Both gas and electric utilities spend time discussing any safety-related events, such as motor vehicle incidents, OSHA recordable events, near misses, or "good catches" by field operations teams, and so much more.

I learned this process well by watching my leaders. Some were great at it, and those were the leaders I learned to emulate. Others instilled a sense of punitive authority that I quickly learned not to replicate in my own career. Most leaders who move up the leadership ladder ask inquisitive questions, often challenging norms and learning from mistakes. But we must be careful not to become so focused on improved performance that we forget about our people, the most valuable asset we have.

While I believe that strong leaders are good at asking questions, quickly assessing risk, and driving the team toward resolution, without a fundamental emphasis on people and safety, we will fail at engaging our people and driving the appropriate behaviors across our companies. As I previously mentioned, great leaders must recognize this important concept of "placing people and safety at the heart of everything we do," driving greater enjoyment, better employee engagement, and, ultimately, cementing the legacy we leave behind.

WHAT DOES SAFETY MEAN?

Make no mistake about it: companies that do not have a passion for safety will rarely realize their full potential. When a high standard of care is not a priority, failures will occur without an understanding of what went wrong.

The most complex problems contain a variety of variables. These are often the most challenging to solve, but when you are able to bring all the pieces together for a solution, it can be incredibly rewarding. Similarly, safety is a multivariable equation; there's no one thing that makes safety happen. Instead, we must listen to employees, track and trend the information we've gathered, learn, adjust our actions, and continuously improve. Seeing the end result can be rewarding, knowing that the solution came not from one person but through the collaboration and support of an entire team.

After working for three large companies that have recovered from tragic incidents, I have learned that there are three types of companies. Think about your own company and place yourself in one of the following scenarios. What's important is not the scenario where your company is now, but what you are willing to do to maintain that position or what you will do to get out of it.

Scenario 1: The company had a tragic incident and has learned from the incident.
Scenario 2: The company had a tragic incident and hasn't learned from the incident.
Scenario 3: The company hasn't had a tragic incident yet.

As you might have guessed, the difference between scenario one and scenario two is a learning culture. Companies that become passionate about learning are less likely to repeat the same mistakes over and over again. An important part of a learning culture is owning what occurs during our time as leaders. The difference between owning what happened and finding an excuse to tell the public is typically the difference between the companies that come out on top and those that continue to make the same mistakes.

I arrived in California in the fall of 2012, approximately a year and a half after the San Bruno incident. A thirty-inch natural gas pipeline had ruptured, devastating Northern California and deteriorating the already fragile trust of Californians in PG&E. Today, the portion of the line that erupted and was displaced is kept by PG&E at its training center, a lasting reminder to those who lost their lives that day, the lessons learned, and the continuous reminder of why safety must always be first. A thorough NTSB investigation later showed that there were a variety of failures that led to the event. During my first week on the job, I realized that the environment was unlike any other I had worked in. Everyone was on a mission to recover from this tragic event, and decisions were made quickly to ensure that it would never happen again.

Through my discussions with employees and other leaders, I was able to assess what had happened in San Bruno from an engineering perspective. More importantly, they shed light on the previous leadership culture that failed to listen to employees. Despite receiving numerous warnings and witnessing various events, the leadership had failed to act.

While there, I encountered amazing employees willing to give their best each and every day. What they needed was leadership to support them and help them get through this horrible time. Instead of pointing to flaws, I pointed to strengths and empowered them to see for themselves where we needed to be better.

Years later, I was tasked by Nick Stavropoulos with helping to develop our leadership tagline for our yearly all-leader meeting. It read, "Do it safely, the right way, as one team, or not at all." The tagline was not created for Wall Street; in fact, it was focused on describing our journey since San Bruno and the work that was still in front of us. We understood our purpose and cultivated an environment where every employee had the opportunity to speak up.

We were able to achieve our goals and objectives with the help of our people. With their buy-in, our safety metrics soared to new levels, and there was a passionate emphasis on learning. An entire book could be written on how to lift a company up after a horrible tragedy, but the learnings can be summarized into three unique sayings that roamed the halls of our California offices: "We can't fix what we don't know about," "Find it—Fix it," and "CAP it."

These three sayings can have powerful impacts on the way we work in any industry. The first speaks to getting our employees to speak up and share what is needed to make meaningful changes. The second is about looking for the things that have been left stranded and unfixed, sometimes for years, and being the leaders who finally resolve the problems our employees need fixed. And finally, the third speaks to creating a historical record of what has been broken so that ownership can be established and solutions can be tracked to completion, not on promises but on meaningful action.

STARTING THE SAFETY JOURNEY

We Can't Fix What We Don't Know About

Every weekday morning, we conducted a safety-focused leadership call known as the Daily Morning Call, as previously mentioned. On this call, we encouraged employees to speak up, often reciting the phrase, "We can't fix what we don't know about." Employees were prompted to share what they needed and where the issues were without fear of getting in trouble so that we could improve as a team. We wanted to make sure that we knew what was going on across the organization. We covered safety, damages to our facilities, motor vehicle incidents, gas supply demands, outages to our pipelines, and one of my favorite metrics, make safe times.

The make-safe statistic changed the way we looked at gas releases associated with damage to our gas pipelines. Instead of only tracking when we arrived at the location of the incident, we tracked how quickly we could safely shut the gas off. This metric was essential in helping our teams understand that making the environment safe was important. The morning call revolutionized the way our gas business ran, a concept that I have continued to reproduce and champion throughout my career at other companies. Creating space and opportunities for employees to alert leadership to problems is an essential part of safety.

Once the leadership learns of an issue, it requires a response. That's where the next step comes in: Find it—Fix it.

Find it—Fix it

Alaska Air had introduced a Corrective Action Program, a system by which any employee could submit concerns, issues, and opportunities. Employees could utilize a digital platform to report what was on their minds. We adopted this strategy after visiting their Washington corporate headquarters, tailored it to our business, and rolled out our own CAP program. Along with what we had learned from our own nuclear facility, we rolled down the path of launching our CAP program.

Our mantra quickly became "Find it—Fix it" to reinforce to employees that we needed their support to find the issues that were hidden within such a large company. Before we knew it, employees were telling us about process and records issues and opportunities to enhance our culture. Our CAP program became a way to understand employee struggles, questions, and areas where they needed help solving problems.

I no longer had to wait for the yearly survey, which was often outdated by the time I received the results. "Find it—Fix it" gave the gift of feedback from our employees, and we showed our appreciation by giving them the support they needed.

It was about finding problems and fixing them promptly to show employees we cared and that their voices were being heard. Once we established a culture of speaking up, followed by a culture of fixing what we found, it was time to mature the CAP program.

CAP It

We had built the CAP application, where employees could enter their concerns, which were reviewed each and every day. No longer was feedback getting lost in email; employees now had an opportunity to share their concerns and receive prompt feedback, all while watching their issues get resolved with full transparency.

"CAP it" was vital in helping us address safety issues early and often. These principles allowed our company to be nationally recognized for our safe pipeline operations.

As leaders, it's important that we empower our teams with the tools and support they need to do their jobs well while maintaining a high standard of care. Our mobile app helped revolutionize how we were doing business and gave employees more ownership to solve problems.

When issues arise in your business, what systems do you have in place to track them? And does your team have the resources they need to solve problems when they arise?

THE RULE OF FIVE

As I reflect on my career, two priorities have consistently guided my leadership: people and safety. Those principles were further strengthened when I joined another exceptional organization, one where the culture was strong, the people were deeply committed, and the work truly mattered. It was an incredible place to work, driven by talented individuals united around a shared purpose: delivering reliable electric power, a vital service that supports the daily lives and economic strength of the State of Arizona.

In this role, I transitioned from the gas business into the electric utility sector, supporting power generation facilities across Arizona and New Mexico. Stepping into this new and demanding position is where I learned the *Rule of Five*: the discipline of identifying and relentlessly focusing on the few priorities that matter most. I relocated my family to Phoenix, Arizona, to take on a role that was both demanding and deeply rewarding, requiring extensive travel and coordination across multiple assets under my project team's responsibility. The experience further sharpened my ability to lead through complexity while staying grounded in what drives results and protects the people behind the work.

I had a great leader named Conrad, who quickly took a liking to me and became a mentor. During one of our meetings, he asked me to shut the door of his office. He put his feet on the desk and asked, "William, what are the five most important things in your life?"

I was initially taken aback, unsure what answer he wanted to hear. But then I answered from the heart and said, "God, my wife Hili, my boys, my extended family, and work."

He said, "Great, I want to teach you something you can't ever forget. Never let the first three items falter, but I need to tell you that the other two will always be in a constant battle for balance." I have come to call this the Rule of Five, recognizing that the first three items on the list will never be sacrificed, while the remaining two items will continue to be a constant balance in my life that I have to continuously balance and give myself grace for not constantly delivering.

I have also built a Rule of Five list as an executive at the companies I've had the privilege to serve. My three main items will always be people, safety, and compliance (our ticket to dance or our price of admission to operate), and I recognize that I will always have to balance so much more of what it takes to run a utility. I have learned that if I can place the top three items at the forefront, the rest will take care of themselves.

When I started at PG&E, we had made tremendous progress but were just beginning to see the fruits of our labor. There were many challenges ahead of us, but placing people and safety first would prove to be the foundation on which we would build our strategies.

GET TO WORK:

1. How consistently am I modeling a safety-first mindset, in both my words and my actions?
2. Have I created an environment where my team feels physically, emotionally, and psychologically safe to speak up and take ownership?
3. What systems, behaviors, or blind spots in my organization could be putting people or trust at risk, and what am I doing to address them?

8

WHEN YOU'RE RIGHT, YOU CAN'T BE WRONG

"Trust in the LORD with all your heart and lean not on your own understanding; in all your ways submit to him, and he will make your paths straight."
Proverbs 3:5–6 NIV

The leadership we work under—and choose to support—inevitably leaves a mark on us. Whether we realize it in the moment or only in hindsight, leaders shape our standards, our confidence, and our understanding of what is possible. The best leaders elevate us: they model integrity, create clarity in uncertainty, and challenge us to grow beyond what we thought we were capable of. Their influence often becomes the blueprint for how we show up for others.

I hope you've had the opportunity to experience that kind of leadership—leadership that invested in you, trusted you, and set the bar high with both expectation and care. Those experiences don't just shape careers; they shape character. They quietly inform how you listen, how you decide, and how you lead today, passing forward what was first poured into you.

I also recognize that finding great leaders is a rare gift. Outside of the tremendous role models my parents have been and the immense support I have received from my wife, Hilary, I have been blessed to have served under one of those genuinely great leaders.

Research shows that this type of leadership is uncommon. According to a recent Gallup survey, **only thirty-six percent of employees believe their company would "do what is right" if they raised a concern.**[1]

As mentioned previously, I met Nick Stavropoulos in late 2012 at PG&E. He started with PG&E in 2011, after the San Bruno incident event had devastated Northern California.

He had joined the company with over thirty-five years of service, which stretched both domestically and internationally. A native New Englander who had spent his entire career supporting gas companies, Nick was a visionary who had seen it all within the utility space. He had learned to embrace tough challenges and weather storms, and his assignment at PG&E would serve as yet another testament to his will and passion for people and safety. His experience served him well as he faced new challenges, pulling from his bag of tools to

---

1. Marco Nink, "Want a Company with More Integrity? Leaders Set the Tone," Gallup, December 14, 2020, https://www.gallup.com/workplace/327521/company-integrity-leaders-set-tone.aspx.

embrace adversity and drive the company to a better place after one of the industry's worst pipeline events.

Nick was engaging, and his Boston accent was hard to miss as it wafted down the hallways of our office in San Ramon, California. He made it a point to connect with as many people as possible, and each conversation served as an opportunity to gain insight into their lives and what was happening within our company. He had restacked our floors, ensuring that all leaders, regardless of title, had a collaborative workspace. He expected his leaders to have an open cubicle where no one had to knock on a door and followed suit by having a cubicle as well. No fancy offices, no hierarchy to walk through to bring issues up; everyone had a voice that could be heard by top leadership.

Our monthly leadership meeting was known as "Keys to Success," an all-day meeting that would provide us with insight into all the work that was happening across our California service territory. We discussed people, safety, compliance, quality, finances, growth, vision, strategy, and challenges facing California. Best of all, it was an opportunity to praise the great work happening throughout the entire leadership team, what we often called "ripples of joy." During this meeting, barriers were removed, gracious accountability took place, and we learned how to get better as one team.

It was here that I heard Nick utilize the saying that has stuck with me for years: "When you're right, you can't be wrong!"

At first glance, that statement might sound like stubbornness or pride. But Nick didn't mean charging ahead on emotion or ego. What he meant aligns closely with Proverbs 3:5–6: *"Trust in the LORD with all your heart and lean not on your own understanding; in all your ways submit to him, and he will make your paths straight."* Being "right" means you've done the hard work; you've gathered the facts, asked the tough questions, listened to wise counsel, dug into the details, and checked your motives. You've prayed, submitted your decision to the Lord, and aligned your actions with what is right before God.

In those moments, when you have truly done your homework and submitted your way to the Lord, you can stand firm. That doesn't mean you'll always be popular. It may be lonely, and it may be costly. But you can move forward knowing you are doing the right thing, trusting that God is the one who will make your path straight.

In my own life, I've had to face tough situations, and Nick's example has continued to resonate with me. Recognizing when we are right or wrong is a skill that we must constantly practice. We've all had leaders who can't admit they are wrong. When that happens, trust is diminished, and we determine that the leader is not worth following. According to a survey conducted by Dale Carnegie Training across 3,100 employees, "Admitting when they are wrong" was rated by eighty-one percent of respondents as "important or very important" to inspiring them to do their best work, yet only forty-one percent said their supervisors could be trusted to do it consistently.

How many business decisions are lost today because one or more parties cannot recognize that they are wrong about an issue or decision? And just as importantly, how many opportunities fail to mature because a leader is unwilling to stand up and defend what they know is right?

Of course, this principle is not a one-sided approach to problems. In fact, the foundational building block is recognizing that we must be balanced and open to the fact that we don't have all the answers. But in certain opportunities in life, our legacy will be defined by staying true to what we know is right!

My commitment to myself has been to go through life without regrets, especially when I am given the opportunity to stand for what is right. The higher we move up the ladder of leadership, the more we need to be aware and decisive about the decisions that will make or break our companies. We must be certain of who we are and how we face problems. This knowledge will help us stand up for our people while making sound business decisions.

BEING RIGHT

We aren't in leadership positions to dance around decisions. When we move higher up in a company, we are trusted and counted on to make very tough calls in what often feels like an expedited manner. Often, leaders must quickly make decisions and rely on sound facts, knowledge, and experience, especially in difficult situations.

"When you're right, you can't be wrong" is not about making wild decisions off the cuff. It's about making decisions even when others influence us to take an opposing view that we know does not align with the facts or the path that needs to be taken.

We can all think of times when we've made decisions knowing that there was little to no risk in being wrong. Making decisions when the entire leadership team is backing us up is easy. But what do we do when that's not the case? It was Abraham Lincoln who said, "It often requires more courage to dare to do the right than to fear to do the wrong." When we step into this mindset, we are choosing to boldly lead a legacy of courage that can have lasting effects.

I have led large teams at different companies through difficult recovery processes and have discovered ways to weather these storms. The pattern is simple yet never easy. I've seen it in Nick, myself, and others throughout my career who have made it through difficult situations. The pattern is one that will drive success: seek sound feedback, develop a reliable plan, and stay true to what you say, even if it comes with opposition.

Seeking Sound Feedback

Our employees often have the right answers. In many cases, they have lived with the frustration of not being heard for years. If we listen intently, they will give us the workings of the playbook for success. Once we learn what this playbook is, it is our job to drive these solutions with a solid plan. Our employees are often eager to provide us with sound feedback and ideas, but are we willing to listen?

When Nick arrived at PG&E, he focused on people and safety. He prioritized hearing feedback from employees, union leaders, public officials, contractors, and more, making it clear that he wanted "to do it right," not just make promises. As one union leader put it, "He walks the walk."[2] From the start, Nick made it his mission to ensure that "our family, friends, and coworkers return home safely ... every single day," underscoring that the most important goal was people's safety. And under his leadership, those ideals translated into tangible, verifiable change: PG&E's gas business earned multiple international safety and asset-management certifications, a signal that safety culture had become embedded in how business was done.[3] Under Nick's direction, the "Find it—Fix it" culture didn't become just a slogan; it became the foundation for real and lasting safety and operational excellence.

This commitment became especially critical in 2012, when a group of employees identified that the company had not been leak-surveying its pipelines, a serious compliance and safety lapse rooted in prior corporate culture. Although Nick was not yet at the company when those actions occurred, he took responsibility for changing the culture. Leak surveying leaves little room for error; it can be the difference between finding a

---

2. David R. Baker, "PG&E Executive Believes in Doing It Right," *SFGATE*, August 4, 2012, https://www.sfgate.com/news/article/PG-E-executive-believes-in-doing-it-right-3763526.php.

3. PG&E, "Independent Third-Party Organization Recognizes PG&E's Comprehensive Asset Management System," news release, July 18, 2017, https://investor.pgecorp.com/news-events/press-releases/press-release-details/2017/Independent-Third-Party-Organization-Recognizes-PGEs-Comprehensive-Asset-Management-System/default.aspx.

leak early and repairing it or allowing an unsafe leak to persist, potentially endangering public safety. Under federal regulations from PHMSA, operators are required to conduct routine and documented leakage surveys at specified intervals based on system type, pressure, location class, and risk. These rules are designed to ensure early detection of hazardous leaks and to prevent conditions that could lead to catastrophic failures. PHMSA's intent behind these requirements is clear: consistent leak surveying is one of the most fundamental protections for the public, and failure to perform these surveys represents a breakdown in both regulatory compliance and safety culture.

Because Nick had created a system for seeking sound feedback, he learned of a serious issue that had lingered for years without resolution from prior leadership. After he learned of this problem, he was at a crossroads. Would he do what he knew to be right? Or would he toe the line, doing what other leaders had done before?

The reality is that if you stay with a company long enough, you will have opportunities to challenge the viewpoints of others and impact people's lives. When we seek feedback and notice the cues that our employees are sending us, we can arrive at a crossroads. Do we continue to do what others have done, or are we going to be the leaders they need and help?

Developing a Robust Plan

When he learned of this compliance issue, Nick responded quickly to the information and developed a robust and strategic plan. The first part of the plan was self-reporting this crucial finding. You might assume that this news was received positively by the local regulatory commission. The reality is that it resulted in a $17 million fine for the company. Still, despite this loss, Nick knew that he was right, so he continued along this course of action.

We must recognize that how we communicate with our employees can make the difference between building or losing trust. Nick seized the moment and decided to stand by his decision.

Nick sent an email to the entire company that spoke of his decision to do the right thing, even though there were financial consequences. The email was an honest thank you to those employees who had reported the risk and a confirmation that, although the commission had issued a hefty fine, he was committed to doing the right thing even if it caused the company further penalties and scrutiny. It had been the right thing to do, and his decision set the tone for how he led PG&E for years to come, with integrity and with trust.

Next, Nick and the team developed a simple and effective plan to improve processes, technology, training, and quality-control measures to prevent something like this from happening again. The plan was built by those who knew the work best and required the entire company to lean in to sustain the changes. The lessons could not be forgotten, and the plan ensured that employees had the tools and support to be successful.

Staying True to What You Said

Nick will be the first to tell you that sometimes you are the only person within the leadership team who has your back. You may be the only one who believes and has the conviction to move forward with the decision that you know to be right. We can't do this alone, so the strategy moves from being right to dedicating ourselves to building converts that can join the mission field alongside us.

Before joining PG&E, when Nick was president at KeySpan Energy, a company crew incorrectly tied a high-pressure system to a low-pressure system. This action led to high-pressure gas entering homes, exceeding the design capabilities of the pipeline system. Gas entered some homes unsafely, igniting and injuring two residents.

Nick knew it was the company's fault, and as the executive over KeySpan, he knew he was personally accountable. As he sought counsel on how to handle the media, he was advised not to take accountability or admit that the incident was KeySpan's responsibility. The comfortable thing to do was to listen to legal counsel and the guidance of those he trusted, but as he stepped up to the mic, his mind was made up. It was the company's fault, and he had committed to holding himself personally accountable for the incident. His decision echoed through the company and the communities KeySpan served. The message Nick delivered resonated through time, and he is still remembered as a leader who would not shy away from tough decisions or accountability.

Following his announcement, Nick received positive feedback from internal and external parties. People praised him for not avoiding the problem and passing the blame elsewhere. Nick was praised for his commitment to making those impacted whole and improving the company after the incident. His promise was to keep people safe; he stayed true to his commitment, even though it was the tougher road to take.

Years later, while at PG&E, Nick would once again learn the importance of these lessons, as he encountered many challenges as he worked to turn the culture around in Northern California.

MAKING THE TOUGH DECISIONS

In leadership, it's important to understand our role and recognize that our decisions can have positive or negative impacts on our employees, the public, and those who choose to invest in our companies. I have made a career out of embracing demanding situations, rather than running from them, as well as acting with direction when challenges have come my way. In the utility space, each day means a new decision to make, whether it's a customer-related call that needs attention, a leak in the system that must be made safe, a pressure excursion that requires evaluation to ensure system integrity, or an upstream issue that is placing strain on the system.

Throughout my career, I've had to make decisions that have often been difficult and sometimes unpopular. Still, repeatedly, I've had the chance to look back with colleagues, teammates, and leaders to recognize that such decisions were the right ones to make, even though they didn't feel like it at the time.

No matter the industry you find yourself in, there will come a time when you have to make a difficult decision. When that time comes, pause and ask yourself:

- Are you seeking sound feedback to understand the needs of the organization and the issues that require your attention?
- When you get feedback, are you working with employees and leaders to develop plans to get the company over the mountain of problems? Or are you sitting back, waiting for others to do it?
- Once you've sought feedback, made a plan, and know you are right about the decision, are you moving forward?

Throughout portions of my career, I've had to make the decisions no one wanted to make, even though I recognized that no one would have my back if I was wrong. These decisions built my career and, most importantly, helped me build trust among my team. When I have thought about these questions and been certain that I was right based on the feedback and plan, I've been able to make these decisions with confidence.

APPLICATION

What does "When you're right, you can't be wrong" look like practically? I have applied this principle throughout my career to both big and small decisions.

During a field visit in a small rural town, I met with two technicians to obtain feedback on the work they were performing. As soon as the three-hour visit commenced, both technicians, one after the other, could not stop telling me about what they needed. They showed me how important their tools were and what could be improved. Throughout our conversation, they told me about their lives, families, and love for the work they did. They worked well together, almost as if they had done it for so long that they could read each other's minds.

As I left with a lengthy list of actions, I asked them to give me one thing that I could do in the near term to help them out. They looked at each other, almost asking for permission, and quickly replied, "It would be amazing if we could get some of the tools we've been asking for, but they won't get approved."

I found out that these tools weren't just needed by this team but by teams around the state. These two individuals weren't just speaking for themselves; they were speaking for the entire company; they were speaking for the team. The reality was that in order to get the necessary tools, we needed millions of dollars. Despite the cost, it was hard to deny that these were critical. What the employees were asking for would make their work safer, enhance their ability to identify issues in the system, and ultimately drive a more efficient approach to performing the work.

After receiving this important feedback, I made a plan to get the tools they needed. I approached my peers on the matter and received the canned answer they had given the employees for years: "It's too much money, and the employees really don't need those tools." I wasn't satisfied with that answer. I knew what was right and was determined to stay true to what I said.

After receiving that answer, I returned to the employees and asked them more questions about the business case for getting this done. It's like they had been preparing for these questions for years. They quickly kicked into gear and helped me build a solid plan to execute on their request.

It was clear that the employees needed these tools; without them, employees were being asked to perform work in an unsafe manner. This was a problem that needed to be fixed, and we had a plan to do just that. Eventually, I found the money, and we delivered the tools to the employees through the plan they had built.

Despite delivering on what the employees needed, I didn't hear anything initially. Months later, I was in the field once again with a different group of employees and leaders, and as I introduced myself, one of the employees said, "You're the guy that got us the tools." I was shocked that the decision I had made months ago had such a positive ripple effect on the organization.

In this situation, I knew that I was right after seeking feedback from employees. Together, we developed a plan to get them what they needed, even though it was costly. And because I stayed true to what I said, the organization and employees benefited.

As leaders, we don't make tough decisions rashly or to inflate our ego: we do it to serve those we are leading. When we take the time to do this, we are leading a legacy that stretches beyond what we can see.

DRIVING EXCELLENCE IN LEADERSHIP

Leaders aren't always given all of the tools or information to make decisions, yet decisions still need to be made in an effort to move the company in the appropriate direction. It's easy to be a leader when all the facts are clearly laid out in perfect order, but that's rarely the case. Instead, we have to rely on those we trust to provide sound guidance, look at the facts we do have, and trust our experience and knowledge to help chart a path forward.

The decisions we make should never be about being right; they should be based on driving excellence in the work we perform. We drive excellence in our organization by making decisions that are grounded in feedback, facts, and the best possible outcome for people and safety.

"When you're right, you can't be wrong" is a reminder to do the right thing even in the face of opposition. It's a call to do good for others, even when it's inconvenient. And it's an opportunity to lead a legacy focused on the right things, which will have a lasting positive impact.

GET TO WORK:

1. Am I delivering the right message in the right way, or is my need to be right getting in the way of building trust and alignment?

2. When disagreement arises, do I listen actively and seek understanding before offering my perspective?
3. Do I have the wisdom to know when to pause and the courage to speak up when doing what's right truly matters?

9

WHEN TROUBLE HITS, AND IT WILL...

"Consider it pure joy, my brothers and sisters, whenever you face trials of many kinds, because you know that the testing of your faith produces perseverance. Let perseverance finish its work so that you may be mature and complete, not lacking anything."
James 1:2–4 NIV

D id you know that some of the highest risks faced by private pilots are the very same risks commercial pilots encounter, just on a larger scale? Ask any airline, and they will tell you that one of the riskiest times for a pilot is when the plane is landing or taking off. This is a critical time when pilots must have their full attention to enter busy airways while tracking weather, turbulence, and congested skies. In recent years, we've seen through media reports that many accidents occur during these moments, often due to a combination of complexity, pressure, and reduced margin for error.

Pilots prepare for this reality through repetition. They practice again and again, spending valuable time in the seat, learning how the aircraft responds and what it takes to execute a safe landing or takeoff. Training prepares pilots to perform safely even when things don't go as planned.

Studies consistently show that most serious commercial aviation accidents occur during takeoff, initial climb, approach, and landing, rather than during cruise. During takeoff and the initial climb, pilots experience a high workload. They must manage landing gear, flaps, power settings, noise abatement procedures, and communication with air traffic control, all while the aircraft remains at low altitude. At this stage, there is very little margin for error. Engine failures, bird strikes, or loss of control can occur quickly.

During approaches and landings pilots must configure the airplane, manage speed, adjust flaps and landing gear, communicate with the tower, and follow precise procedures, all while close to the ground. Many accidents during this phase are linked to unstable approaches, hard landings, runway excursions, or poorly executed go-arounds. By contrast, the cruise phase of flight sees far fewer accidents, largely because pilots have time, altitude, and space to think.

Data from the FAA and NTSB show that a disproportionate number of accidents occur in the first and last ten to fifteen minutes of flight, even though those minutes represent only a small fraction of total flight time. That's why airlines emphasize intense focus during these critical phases and why I've spent years taking my teams to learn from them. Their approach to preparation and discipline is a model worth studying.

What is true for pilots is also true for leaders: trouble will hit. The question isn't *if*, but *how* we respond when it does. When pressure comes, we don't panic, hide, or pretend it's easy. Instead, we face trials with a steady, anchored attitude, trusting that God can use the storm to build perseverance, depth, and maturity in our teams and in us.

As leaders, we model this response by staying calm, honest, and hopeful. We help our people see that even in the hardest seasons, something can be formed in us that could not be formed any other way. Preparation today allows us to "land safely" time and time again.

We must accept the reality that trouble will cross our path. If we stop fearing it and start preparing for it, we grow stronger, help others do the same, and develop leaders who step forward when things get hard rather than stepping back.

HANDLING TROUBLE

After watching ExxonMobil, PG&E, NiSource, and several other companies successfully recover after serious events, I have learned how to move successful companies from event to recovery. The timeline is dependent on many factors, but I have seen the process play out numerous times. If these steps are followed, I'm certain that companies can realize success and, more importantly, sustain that success as part of their ongoing company legacy.

I first saw this strategy come to life at PG&E as we laid out our team's line-of-sight vision, a strategic process grounded in people, safety, reliability, compliance, affordability, and the customers we served. It reinforced an important truth: the same Five Keys to Success continue to show up. When we're continuously looking for where those connections come to life, we can simplify our vision to success.

While my experience with this process has been in the utilities space, the journey to recovery is essentially the same across industries. It starts with a commitment at the very top, as well as a steady walk down to each employee and contractor to make the appropriate changes. I have witnessed senior leaders drive this model in different scenarios, sometimes with success and other times in utter failure. Success comes when each step is implemented thoroughly and in order. Failure is often a result of wanting to skip through the important initial steps in order to get to the final step more quickly.

Each phase of this process must be handled diligently; it's not something to be taken lightly. Adequate completion of each step is required to get to a sustainable path that can help our companies achieve even better success. No matter the trouble, recovery can happen with dedication and hard work at every level of the company.

I want to emphasize that a company does not need to experience a tragic or disruptive event to implement the four phases outlined below. In fact, the very steps used to guide an organization through recovery are the same steps I have consistently applied to strengthen, mature, and improve companies operating in steady-state conditions.

While recovery becomes unavoidable at certain points, and leaders who remain in their roles long enough will inevitably face moments of crisis, high-performing leaders do not wait for adversity to act. They proactively evaluate and apply these principles during normal operations, enabling continuous improvement, strengthening resilience, and preventing potential issues from ever escalating into serious incidents.

Below are the four steps to handle trouble and bring a company back to health, as well as continuously improve a company's performance.

Phase I: Year of *Discovery* – "The Voice of Our People"

This period of time is dedicated to figuring out what went wrong, along with anything else that may need attention. I have utilized this time to understand areas of weakness within the company's culture. This step serves as a prime time to seek feedback and understand the needs of employees, customers, and internal and external stakeholders. It is also a time to determine what the leadership structure should look like and how we can operate our business in new and innovative ways.

Listening is paramount in the wake of trouble. This phase centers on the company's needs and listens to the voices that matter most: those who know the work. It is a critical time for senior executives to listen, learn, and plan.

This can be a difficult step for any leader, but it cannot be discounted or passed over. Instead of immediately making changes, first, seek feedback and learn from those around you. A time for action will come, but those actions must be grounded in sound information.

Phase II: Year of *Execution* – "Driving our Commitments"

Our findings come together during this phase to drive the execution of key process changes. Here, we implement appropriate programs to mitigate risk while ensuring that the commitments laid out in Phase I are executed. This is the time to follow through and show stakeholders that their suggestions have led to action. You would be surprised how much trust can be built or rebuilt by this simple act alone.

This is the "back to basics" stage. This phase is the place to ensure that fundamental components of the business are handled with care, minimizing additional risk and managing the organization's needs through appropriate people, processes, and technology.

It can be tempting to breeze through this phase because it's not exciting. But it's your responsibility as a leader to resist that urge. There's a chance that trouble will hit because the basics weren't being followed. This is why rebuilding that foundation of the basics is so important. Before you can innovate, the basics must be sound.

Phase III: Committing to *Excellence* – "Placing Quality at the Source"

In Phase III, we've listened, learned, and executed on our path to turning things around. At this stage, we move from executing on the basics to executing those basics with excellence, learning from those who know what good looks like, and bringing lessons back to our teams.

I utilize this time to bring in external parties that can provide insight into how to improve processes and procedures, as well as introduce additional technology changes. This stage helps us move closer to excellence and, more importantly, helps us build quality at the very source of our work so our employees can rest assured that they have what they need to succeed. During this phase, we develop strong quality metrics, and as a professor in quality and a friend shared with me, it is the opportunity to "place quality at the source," the action of placing quality where the work begins.

In my own experience at two different companies, Phase III was when we achieved our international certifications for safety management. These achievements didn't happen overnight but were the result of years of diligent work done by people at every level of the company.

Excellence will come as a result of hard work. Don't expect results immediately.

Phase IV: Building *Unity and Trust* – "You Can't Ask For It..."

You may have heard the phrase, "Trust can't be asked for. It must be earned." One of the last steps in setting the sustainable culture of a company comes from building unity and trust. This can only happen once the previous phases have been adequately accomplished. Don't share a vision for unity and trust until you are certain the commitments made have been accepted and fulfilled by the organization.

Employees need to know that you are going to do what you said you were going to do. More importantly, they need to know that you will be relentless in listening to and championing their needs and aspirations. After a challenging event, one must find opportunities where employees are struggling each day to do their work well. The foundational items that are typically missing are appropriate staffing, modern tools and technology, and processes. Without these, we place ourselves in a position where employees will not be able to build unity or trust, as these cultural components must first be proven by senior leadership.

Building unity and trust is the foundation for the next stage of an important journey every company must embark on. After trust and unity are built, this focus on efficiency results in the ability to do more essential work at a lower cost. This also improves the financial stability of the company, shareholder value, and our ability as leaders to provide better for our employees. More importantly, this focus on efficiency places more dollars on the table to support the needs of the company to make things safer all around.

TRAINING FOR TROUBLE

I can't help but wonder why the first class in college isn't titled "Trouble Will Hit You." While we don't want to paint a grim picture of life, we do need to describe the reality of what a leader will face. We know that trouble will hit, so how do we train for trouble? How do we allow our leaders to prepare for what will ultimately come?

Trouble can take many forms: a bad financial year due to higher interest rates, a product not delivered on time, a recall that places the company's product at risk, a regulatory or tax change that stresses the balance sheet, a significant error by a well-meaning employee, or a catastrophic event that seems impossible to recover from.

We train for trouble by ensuring that we develop a curious environment throughout our organizations, where the fear of finding trouble is removed and feedback is welcomed and appreciated. At every level, great leaders develop a desire to learn and grow, no matter what comes their way.

I have found it essential to model this behavior within my teams, teaching my leaders that it's okay to bring problems, with an expectation that they will be part of the solution as well. Finding these challenges or problems places us in a position to see what no one else can see.

Over time, I have found joy in seeing opportunities to learn and find examples in everyday life that I can bring back to my leadership team. I look for opportunities at restaurants, construction sites, banking institutions, other utilities, and even my kids' school and our church. What am I seeing that someone else may miss? Where do I see an opportunity that others may not see?

Over the years, I have trained my heart and mind to recognize what "good" looks like. Two examples immediately come to mind.

One simple instance occurred at church one weekend in the area designated for coffee. People would grab their coffee, then get their creamer, and afterward, walk over to the garbage can to throw away their creamer capsules, all the while maneuvering through people, spilling coffee, and scrambling to get to their seats. After several weeks of this, I spoke with the pastor about the possibility of drilling a hole in the counter. This way, when people poured their coffee and creamer, they could simply dump everything into a garbage can positioned underneath. I even tested my theory by placing a cup with used creamer packages on the counter, and as expected, the people behind me started placing their trash in the cup as well, which minimized traffic and allowed them to quickly fill their cups with coffee and creamer.

To me, what "good" looks like means creating a setup that simplifies the process for everyone. I love watching and observing, asking the questions that many may see past.

At work, I listen to investors' calls throughout the country to understand what other companies are encountering; I look for cues from one investor or ways that companies are positioning themselves for success. I look for issues and tones, for opportunities and challenges, and every so often, I witness moments that stick with me and help me understand underlying issues that may not be easily understood if one were to only listen to one company's call.

Once you train your mind to look for what is good, it becomes automatic in all aspects of life. More importantly, as you train your mind, you also train your heart to recognize what good looks like. This shift allows us to view people differently, focusing on their strengths rather than their weaknesses.

Unfortunately, many leaders wake up each day determined to identify what their team members are doing wrong. In doing so, they often overlook the positive contributions being made. Understanding what good looks like involves recognizing what is being done well, learning from those successes, and finding ways to improve upon what already exists. This curious mindset with an eye on finding solutions is what training for trouble is all about. When we turn problems around and look at them from a different viewpoint, we turn challenges into opportunities. And when these opportunities are practiced, we get better at embracing problems.

Companies don't need weak leaders who stand behind problems as excuses not to deliver. And employees certainly don't need leaders who drown in a sea of issues, unable to help them. Training for trouble is an essential part of life, and as leaders, we must never miss an opportunity to embrace a problem that comes our way.

I had the privilege to sit down with the CEO of another utility to chat about safety, people, culture, and a better way to run our businesses. This particular CEO said something that I will continue to carry in my mind forever. She said, "Ask your teams, 'What has to be true for you to solve the problem?'"

What brilliant advice! Instead of asking how to solve the problem or why they can't achieve the necessary outcome, we can choose a better question. Asking our teams to think about what has to be true for the problem to be resolved flips the problem upside down and gets them to think about solutions that we might miss.

We must be solutions looking for a problem, not problems looking for more problems without an end in mind. You've met those who are problems looking for more problems. They come to meetings with a problem and spend their time dwelling on why it can't be fixed, focusing on ideas that won't work and dragging everyone down. Those who are solutions looking for problems recognize that problems are present but live in the art of the possible; they look for solutions and help others see a way out. We need to model the behaviors that we want to see from our teams. It's up to us to teach our leaders and employees to be curious in all situations and look for innovative ways to turn problems into opportunities for success.

We train for trouble by modeling this behavior. Do we lose our minds in chaos when a problem comes, or do we sit with our employees to dissect the problem and help them see a way out? Do we teach them to do this on their own so they can pass it along to their teams?

Like anything else, we have to train this process and drive on a continuous basis. I have countless examples of individuals bringing bad news early to me, opening up discussions about problems when we can fix them rather than waiting until the damage is past the point of no return. Because I have trained my teams for trouble, we are more ready to respond when trouble hits. Our curious and solution-oriented mindset has made it so that we don't just have to survive in trouble, but we can move from trouble to triumph.

TROUBLE TO TRIUMPH

Trouble doesn't always come with flashing lights or warning sirens. Sometimes it shows up as a tragedy, sudden and painful. Other times, it creeps in through financial pressures, cultural fractures, operational failures, or the slow grind of resource constraints. Trouble comes in many forms, but its impact is always the same: it challenges the very core of who we are as leaders.

The defining moments of leadership don't happen when everything is going according to plan. They happen in the storm, when the ground shakes, when the air feels heavy, when people are looking for someone to trust, someone to follow. In those moments, leadership is not about position. It's about presence. It's about stepping forward when others hesitate.

One of the defining moments in my career occurred while I was working in Arizona, watching the aftermath of the San Bruno incident unfold on television. At the time, I was with another company, but I could feel the tremors of what that single incident would mean for our entire industry. It was more than a pipeline failure—it was a cultural reckoning. I knew the consequences would reach far beyond the blast radius. It would reshape how we thought about safety, culture, transparency, accountability, and leadership.

When I arrived at PG&E to support the company during the recovery and transformation process, I was ready—not because I was perfect, but because I had prepared. My early training and my work across field operations, engineering, emergency response, and regulatory environments had laid the foundation. The preparation I received early in my career became the bedrock for everything that followed. I had been training for this moment my whole life.

I remember getting the call. When I ultimately joined the effort, I was honored to serve alongside so many dedicated leaders who gave me guidance and support and employees who helped me understand the work through their own lived struggles. Together, we embraced the challenge, not because it was easy but because it was necessary.

That was the beginning of something that would define much of my career. Again and again, I would be called to enter troubled waters. And again and again, my experience allowed me to serve others, to be the one who reminded people there was a path forward. In times of crisis, I didn't just talk about safety and trust; I demonstrated it. I helped others see light when all they could feel was the weight of darkness.

A leader who has seen trouble doesn't fear future trouble. They embrace it. They don't just stand in the storm; they become a lighthouse for others.

I've dealt with angry customers who needed hope in impossible moments. I've worked with state officials who needed answers for their constituents. I've stood with friends and family who were directly impacted by our work. In every case, the people needed more than policy; they needed someone to care enough to lead them through it.

I've walked into control rooms in the middle of major events: storms, cold weather emergencies, system failures, and so much more. I've sat across from state and federal personnel, regulatory bodies, and oversight teams. I've stood before employees whose morale was shattered and helped them find their purpose again. I've led teams through restructures, crises, lawsuits, and audits, not because I wanted those battles but because I was called to serve in them.

And while I've had the privilege to lead, I remain deeply thankful to God for the trouble He allowed me to walk through—not to punish, but to prepare me. Without the hardships, I wouldn't have the depth to lead. Without the struggles, I wouldn't have the strength to stay.

I often tell my teams, "When you're in a storm, don't focus on what's out of your control. Focus on your anchor." That anchor might be your values, your training, your people, or even your faith. It's what keeps you grounded when everything else is shifting.

Trouble doesn't show up politely. Sometimes it's gradual, sometimes it's instant, but it always asks the same question: Are you ready?

Oscar Munoz was. When he became CEO of United Airlines, he inherited an organization strained by operational failures, poor morale, and public frustration. And just one month into his role, he suffered a near-fatal heart attack. Most people would've stepped aside, but Munoz didn't. He returned with clarity and compassion and rebuilt the company, not just structurally but also culturally. His leadership brought stability, humanity, and humility to a company that desperately needed all three.

So was Alan Mulally. When he walked into Ford during the financial collapse, the company was bleeding billions and paralyzed by internal silos. He didn't issue ultimatums; he unified people. He simplified the strategy. He restored belief. Under his leadership, Ford didn't just survive; it became a case study in turnaround success.

Howard Schultz, returning to Starbucks amid a global recession, found a company that had lost its soul. He didn't flinch. He closed stores, retrained baristas, and recentered the company around its core values. He placed people back at the center of the experience and reignited a culture of excellence.

And consider Mary Barra. In her very first year as CEO of General Motors, she was confronted with a deadly ignition switch crisis that had been buried for years. It could have destroyed trust and derailed her leadership, but she didn't hide. She confronted the issue, took accountability, changed the culture, and reshaped GM's commitment to safety and ethics. Her leadership wasn't reactive; it was transformative.

We've also seen leaders who have drawn on their faith, experience, and passion to lead their teams through darkness into success. These stories aren't just moments of professional triumph—they reflect a deeper purpose. These leaders modeled what it looks like to lead a legacy, a theme that runs throughout this book. Each one chose to be more than reactive; they chose to be redemptive.

And yet, not everyone responds this way.

I've seen people who looked unstoppable on paper but who crumbled when adversity arrived. Their resumes were impressive, their credentials polished, but when the pressure hit, they folded. And worse, they left no positive legacy behind. Why? Because what was under the hood wasn't a spirit of legacy, but a structure never built on a solid foundation. And when the storms came, it all collapsed. There was nothing left for others to model, remember, or be inspired by.

In contrast, I've watched my own teams face adversity and rise, not with ego but with unity. In hardship, they leaned into each other. They weren't concerned about which one of them would take my place when the time came. Instead, they understood that the true measure of character would be how they showed up together. In challenging times, those same teams worked as one, lifting each other up, solving problems as a unit, and remaining unshakable in the face of overwhelming obstacles.

That's leadership.

Leadership isn't loud. It's consistent. It's humble. It's sacrificial. It's being the one others trust when the lights go out.

So, if you're facing a storm right now—whether personal, professional, financial, or spiritual—know this: you were made for this. You're not being punished; you're being prepared. And your ability to lead through this moment will give others permission to believe, to hope, and to move forward with courage.

Don't just survive trouble; embrace it.

Don't just manage the darkness; light the way through it.

Be the lighthouse.

Because when trouble hits, your team, your company, and your community will look to you. And if you've done the work, if you've trained your heart and mind, if you've placed people and safety at the heart of everything you do, you'll be ready.

And one last thing: Don't look for a job that masks stress or promises to be trouble-free. Such a job doesn't exist; even if it did, it wouldn't contribute to your growth. Look for the job that challenges you, that tests you, that shapes you. Because in the midst of that challenge, you'll discover something far greater than comfort: purpose.

You may not enjoy the trouble, but you will come to value the trust others place in you to be the lighthouse in their storm.

When trouble hits, lead.

When trouble hits, serve.

When trouble hits, believe.

When trouble hits, be the light.

And most of all, be the leader who is set apart for this moment. Learn to embrace it. Face what's ahead. Be the leader who trains others to weather the storms that lie ahead.

GET TO WORK:

1. Train before the storm. Build a solid foundation through values, experiences, and preparations so you are ready when a crisis hits.
2. Lead as a lighthouse. In adversity, show up with clarity and courage to guide others through uncertainty.
3. Strengthen the team. Foster unity and resilience so your team can face hardships together, not alone.

10

THE BAG OF TOOLS

"If the axe is dull and its edge unsharpened, more strength
is needed, but skill will bring success."
Ecclesiastes 10:10 NIV

W hile the four phases of recovery provide a strategic roadmap for navigating organizational storms, even the best plan is only as strong as the person standing behind it. Preparing for trouble is the "flight manual" of leadership, but eventually, you will encounter a moment where the manual ends and your character begins.

It's a perfect picture for everyday leadership: your "tools" are your character, your skills, your judgment, and your relationships. If you don't keep them sharp through learning, reflecting, getting feedback, and growing with others, you end up working harder, pushing more, and still getting less impact. However, daily investment in sharpening these tools, particularly through "iron sharpens iron" relationships, as mentioned in Proverbs 27:17, enhances the effectiveness, precision, and sustainability of your leadership over time. In the following pages, I have listed some of my favorite tools and leadership thoughts that serve as a reminder of what our actions and words should be. Some of these tools I've discovered on my leadership journey, and others I borrowed from mentors who have helped shape me over time.

You will find anecdotes to encourage you, life lessons to help you get through the week, and leadership fundamentals that will come in handy over time. My desire is that these tools, tips, thoughts, and actions inspire and help you as you lead a legacy. Revisit this chapter again and again to find the right tool for whatever situation you are facing. I have repeated some tools within this section of the book to make it easier for you to find.

LEADERSHIP

Lead a Legacy Each Day

There's no better way to live than knowing that you are making a difference and finding joy in what you are doing. Leading a legacy involves not only influencing the future but also inspiring others.

On a plane ride, I sat next to a leader for The Ohio State University's endowment program who shared stories of regular individuals, not those who were born wealthy or worked high-profile jobs, but those who simply wanted to lead a legacy. He spoke of an elderly woman who decided to leave $4 million to the University of Arizona's Opera Program, a school he had previously supported and my alma mater. He said, "She remembered struggling, searching for her opera dream, and wanted others to have the support they needed."

He also spoke of a donor who owns an NBA team and understood that his legacy wouldn't just be his accomplishments; it was much more important for his daughters to know that giving back was the ultimate legacy.

Leading a legacy drives us. Wake up each day with purpose, knowing what your legacy looks like. It will go too fast; seize today.

> **TIP:** Everyone will leave a legacy, but few will actively *lead* a legacy. Will you lead a positive legacy? Write down what you want your legacy to be, look at it each month, and set goals that get you there.

Find Praising Moments

Keep your eyes wide open for those serving your organization each day. Search for the individuals who give their absolute best, praise them, and grow them. Each day, you should have a healthy tension in your heart and mind, which asks you if you've praised those around you enough. Now that I've trained myself, I am constantly reminded of this tool. I have become a PR representative for my team, finding opportunities to advocate for the work they do.

Praising moments are everywhere; they happen during calls, meetings, elevator rides, field visits, email conversations, and even when things don't go as planned. I have found that most employees show up wanting to give their absolute best. They take pride in doing their jobs correctly, and it's our privilege to praise them.

As an example, I take time to read each comment that my team and I receive during our yearly employee engagement surveys, and once received the following anonymous feedback from a frontline employee: "I was struggling through a mistake I made, and William called me and said, 'This too shall pass.'"

I remembered the call. The employee had made a significant mistake, one that we could have prevented if we had the right controls. But before reacting, I thought about how I would have felt if the issue hinged on me. I called the employee and let him know that we had failed as a leadership team and that we needed better processes. The call didn't require much from me, but hearing from me was exactly what he needed.

Find moments to praise and encourage; you have great people giving you their best each day. Moments to praise are invaluable and can make an immense impact on those around you. The more employees you have, the more attentive you will need to be with how you use this tool. As my teams grew from less than one hundred to over three thousand, I started changing my approach. Each month, I call as many employees as possible on their work anniversaries, thank and praise them for their contributions, and slip in a feedback session that allows me to find out what's going on. Sometimes my calls are random across the organization, and they serve as a great opportunity to hear the voice of the organization. You would be amazed at how helpful these calls can be.

> **TIP:** Figure out what works for your team and scale it as needed.

The Five Most Important Words

After my eldest son's last game, the coach spoke to all of the parents. His message hit me harder than most messages I've heard from professional executive coaches and public speakers.

He said a study was done years ago about the most powerful words we can tell our kids after a good or a bad game. The coach recounted, "The study found that the five most important words you can tell your children after a game are, 'I love watching you play,'" and I haven't looked at leadership the same way since.

As leaders, it's our job to coach, provide support, and help our team through growth, challenges, and mistakes. We play as we practice, and when we know our teams have practiced, we must accept that the results may not be what we expect. Our results on game day are often a representation of how we coached and grew the team. It's a mirror that turns right back at us.

Let's learn to love watching our teams play.

Good leaders are there to teach, mentor, guide, coach, and more. Good leaders also know when to sit back and watch the team play. Corporate America also has "game days," such as board meetings, public outreach events, executive meetings, incidents, all-hands, employee visits, challenges, and more. Look for "game days," watch your team play, and acknowledge their effort.

> **TIP:** Sometimes it's not time to teach, mentor, guide, or coach; it's simply time to say, "I love watching you play."

Create Value

Leaders can't expect to just reap the benefits from someone else's hard work. We can be thankful for the legacy that someone has left, but we must add value.

I once asked the CEO of a major gas utility, "Do you lead the company in the same manner as when you started as CEO, or have you changed your approach over time?"

He said, "Value is created from driving the core of the business well while ensuring that the company stays active in driving sustainable change. When I started, I told everyone that I didn't know much about the gas industry, so we were going to look different because I was going to change some things. Now that I've been here for a number of years, we have moved from change to stability." My friend learned to create value from the experiences he brought from outside of the gas industry, and we must understand how we, too, can create value as we grow in our roles.

Leaders must always find ways to add value. Any time I've been given a new role, I have learned to see the value someone left behind while improving the business. I have created value every step of the way and have passed this skill to all my leaders. I have then witnessed those leaders become supervisors, managers, and directors of organizations and create their own legacies through their passion.

Ask yourself, *am I creating value by finding a better way? Or have I gotten comfortable with the success of the past?* Be intentional in sharpening your skills and contributions.

> **TIP:** Look for ways to energize your team through the wheel of continuous improvement.

Be a Solution Looking for a Problem

I've met people who are problems looking for more problems. These are people who seek to dump issues into the laps of others—the typical "dump and run."

We want to create organizational cultures in which people

question problems and aren't afraid to do so, even when it's not popular.

When we are "a solution looking for a problem," we become individuals who live in the world of the possible. With this mindset, we understand how to find the fifty ways why something won't work, but more importantly, we know how to find the one reason why it will work. The art of looking for problems gets flipped upside down when we do it with a mindset that knows the end goal is a solution.

Lead, knowing it's possible! Be a leader who looks for a way out of the problem. Those who work with me know that we bring our problems to the table, get them out, provide healthy pushback, and find solutions!

> **TIP:** Invite an open mindset, look for problems, and train yourself to find solutions. Never dump the problem in someone's lap and wait for them to solve it.

Know What Made You

Place your title in this statement: *Know what made the* _____ (business professional, doctor, banker, teacher, pastor, architect, welder, construction worker, executive, etc.).

We must know what made us, as these subtle differences help us understand how to handle situations and, more importantly, how we will react in difficult times. I know I was made by a family that showed me a passion for people and safety. I was formed by a deep respect for the communities where we live and a shared responsibility to protect the environment for future generations. Those principles are a few of the components that have made me, that have made this engineer passionate about what matters most.

After reading this book, you now have my perspective on some of the things that made this engineer. I'm proud to be an American while also being honored to have been born in Panama; I love the unique perspective I have from these two very different worlds. I grew up behind the yoke of a plane and behind the wheel of things mechanical. But most importantly, I grew up on the bedrock of a loving family and a God who has never failed me. I grew up with a love for all types of people and watched a constant example of that through my parents and family. You have your own story that you can pull from to help your team succeed. When you understand what made you, you can find your strengths and use them to drive your career. Don't wait too long to figure this out; start knowing what made you today.

> **TIP:** Understand where you came from, what made you, and why you are the way you are. Engage in a constant process of learning. Knowing who you are will help you understand why you do what you do and how you can do it better.

Intellectual Curiosity

There is an innate principle that is far more important than any procedure we can ever write, any safety meeting we can ever host, or any training we can ever have: intellectual curiosity. If we could mentor each of our employees down the road of curiosity, we would create one of the most powerful tools within our organizations.

Intellectual curiosity is about creating a culture where every employee comes into work asking some key questions:

- What can go wrong?
- How bad could it be?
- How often could it happen?
- What controls do I have in place?
- Are those controls sufficient, or do I need additional controls?

Intellectual curiosity involves thinking not just about your day but about the days of others and understanding what's around you. It requires developing a mindset that is curious about everything that happens around you and, therefore, drives much better results. This not only applies to safety; these questions should be asked within all aspects of our business. A leader who trains a culture where employees have intellectual curiosity will train an organization that understands and balances all types of risk.

Start creating curiosity in your organization today. Be a leader who talks about this, trains this, and encourages a curious mindset that never stops thinking about being better.

If you find yourself doing the same thing each day without figuring out what it takes to be better, you haven't developed the intellectual curiosity needed to maintain that edge. Stretch that muscle.

TIP: Be curious about your job and teach others to look for ways to be curious.

If You Can't Change the People, Change the People

This phrase has helped me make some of the best and most challenging decisions in my career. We want to believe that every individual in our organization is cut out for the work, but the reality is that the journey is not for everyone.

Early in my career as a leader, I was helping to mentor and coach a young man whose performance had been declining. I met with him several times to understand his ambitions, the challenges he faced, and the areas of opportunity. After evaluating his performance for a month or so, I decided that the best step as his new leader was to put him on a performance improvement plan.

As we sat down, I handed him his performance improvement plan, and before I started going through it, I saw a grin on his face that I will never forget. He had already made his decision. What I hadn't realized was that over the last month of my mentorship, he had come to understand that he was in the wrong place, the wrong job. This young man pulled out his resignation letter, handed it to me, and thanked me. We are still in touch to this day, and I've watched him flourish in his new career.

Sometimes, it's time to train the employees and help them gain the skills they need to succeed. Other times, an employee is a wrong fit, and it's time for a change.

> **TIP:** Reward the top performers and manage performance where needed; face it head-on.

Be Timeless

Are your actions today allowing you to conquer the small hill ahead of you? Or are you making decisions that will sustain the company for the long run?

We need both, but it can be easy to get caught up in the day-to-day and pay little attention to what's five, ten, and even fifteen years ahead. Although it's hard to get people to think years ahead, challenge your teams to think about long-term outcomes rather than only looking at short-term effects. Thinking ahead can help produce timeless solutions.

A timeless leader isn't moved by every trend or fad. This type of leader drives strategies that stretch beyond today or tomorrow; they carry companies to places where others can only dream. Timeless leaders listen to others and take time to look ahead. Their strategies remain timeless, not perfect, but timeless.

My vision for my team has been to place people and safety at the heart of everything we do, be compliant in our operations, drive quality in our work, and be good financial stewards of the funds entrusted to us. That legacy has become timeless within the companies I've served and has allowed me to stay ahead of changing trends and opportunities. The leader who paints a timeless vision can then embark on the other components to help sustain the business through times of change. If we don't get this right, we end up always trying to catch up and never have time to innovate for the future.

> **TIP:** Take small steps to win the hill each day, but don't forget the long-term needs of the company; assume that no one else is thinking about that.

TEAMWORK

Win, Train, Send

As leaders, we never want to get into the grind of hiring people for the company. After I graduated from college, I had one of the most amazing experiences being hired by Exxon. They were welcoming, passionate, and genuinely cared about my success. The moment I met the staff at Exxon, I knew they were doing everything possible to win me over to the company.

While my experiences have varied from company to company, the times when individuals have cared enough to win me to the company have stuck with me. I adopted that philosophy, and it has allowed me to be passionate about winning the best people to my company, training them the right way, and sending them off to be our next leaders and technical experts.

Are you winning people through your culture, your passion, and your ability to paint a vision, or are you simply hiring?

> **TIP:** Are you hiring or winning people to you? Are you training them the way they deserve? Are they becoming the leaders and technical experts you need? If the answer to all of these isn't yes, take some time to reflect on your priorities and processes.

What You Allow is What You Teach

People will rarely commit beyond the leader. Over time, what a leader allows will become the mode of operation. Are you allowing others to behave a certain way through your actions?

As leaders, we don't get a pass. We must always be vigilant and understand that our teams are watching our behaviors. If you allow employees to deviate from the appropriate practices, you are teaching them it's okay. Don't allow it; you are normalizing a problem you will have to fix later.

TIP: Reflect on each problem you face and ask yourself if you're allowing it. If you allowed it, you created it; now you must help your team create change.

Have Fun

It was transformational for me to realize that fun at work is essential. I've always tried to find ways to enjoy my job, but it transforms organizations when we start looking for ways for others to have fun. This goes beyond team-building events or ways to recognize our employees. I'm talking about enjoying the work we do and allowing others to experience the same.

We need to find ways to help employees see that what we do every day makes a difference in the lives of others. When we find ways to have fun, productivity will increase, employees will be more engaged, and you will find greater meaning in the work you've been called to do.

TIP: You typically spend more time with your team than your own family each day. Are you enjoying them, and are they enjoying you? Make them smile, find joy in them, and know that you can do this while leading the highest-performing teams.

Live in the Green, Don't Be Afraid of the Red

When it comes to key performance indicators, I want a Christmas tree; I want reds, greens, and yellows on my team's dashboards.

The beautiful red circles on a graph tell where people need help and support. The yellow circles signal something isn't going great, but my team has a plan to resolve it. The greens are opportunities to say one of the most precious words: "arigato," "obrigado," "spasibo," "tack," "asante," "merci," "dankie," "kiitos," "gracias," or just a simple "thank you"!

We must train our teams to live in the green without ever being afraid to give us the reds. That's when magic happens, culture expands, and we get to see behind the veil.

> **TIP:** Thank your team for bringing you problems, and praise them regardless of which color they bring to you.

DRIVING EXCELLENCE

Safety Always Wins

Everything will compete with safety, but safety must always win. As you move up in an organization, you will be pressed to move budgets around, make decisions based on limited facts, or have investors who would like to see higher profit margins. Remember that safety must always win.

Neglecting a high standard of care has tremendous repercussions for any company. Therefore, we must always remind ourselves that everything will try to compete with safety, including budgets, internal and external stakeholders, investor earnings, and more. As leaders, we have a responsibility to protect our people and the public.

Realize that when it gets tough, you must be tough enough to follow through on your convictions. Create a culture where people can challenge you, but always ensure that safety wins.

> **TIP:** Everything will compete with safety, but safety must always win.

Drive Balanced Change Continuously

Change is necessary in every company, but it can be difficult to get right. As leaders, we must continuously drive balanced changes so that our teams stay relevant and innovative. Teams often fall into two ruts regarding change: being change-averse or changing too much without balance.

It's easy to wash, rinse, and repeat the cycle of work. We can move almost on autopilot, doing the same thing year after year. If this is the case, it may be time to stop and drive a different vision. If this is where you find yourself, reflect on where you've brought your team, how much they've accomplished, and how much more they could do with a refined vision.

Change is good, but it must be thoughtful and balanced. You can't walk into the office each week with a new vision because you were inspired by a motivational podcast over a great cup of coffee. If you enjoy change, emphasize the importance of balance as you roll out innovative ideas and initiatives.

> **TIP:** Change is important and inevitable. Recognize when it's time to grow and change, and don't miss the next opportunity to change once again. When rolling out change, be sure to keep it balanced!

No Surprises

Does your team know that you expect few or no surprises? We can deal with problems that come to us early, but we can rarely find solutions when the problem has materialized beyond repair. Build a culture where issues are brought up early, and teams are kept in the loop with changing conditions.

Of course, some things will happen outside our control; our teams will be surprised by outside forces, and we may not get the news as early as we want. Have grace here; we aren't aiming for perfection, but improved communication with our teams and internal and external stakeholders.

Set the tone for no preventable surprises. In other words, if we saw it coming, we should communicate about it, never fearing early recognition of a situation.

> **TIP:** Create a culture of identifying potential surprises. Remember that bad news early is wonderful.

Find it—Fix It

"We can't fix what we don't know about," was the saying I heard throughout my time at PG&E.

Your role as a leader is to find and then fix the problems that are keeping you from achieving greatness. Without that, the company does not need you! Are you looking for those pain points, or are you hiding from what needs fixing? Are you searching for the fixes, and are you championing the change that is warranted?

> **TIP:** You can't ask individuals to tell you what needs fixing and then sit back and watch nothing happen. Leaders are here to fix problems. Listen to problems and show your employees that you can fix them.

Drill Deep into the Data

Every company uses data to drive results. As leaders, we have to understand this data to make good decisions that can have long-lasting effects. This is challenging work that requires asking a series of questions to arrive at the appropriate solution. True change comes from our ability to understand what information we have, what information we don't have, and how to interpret the data beyond how it appears on the surface.

This is even easier to do today thanks to AI. We are seeing safer, better, and faster results than we could have imagined, thanks to this new technology. Use the tools available to you to go deep into the data so that you can make better decisions for your team and company.

> **TIP:** Look at all data, understand what it means, and don't assume someone's reading of the data is what we are meant to interpret.

BUILDING CHARACTER

The Rule of Five

Some of the most successful CEOs I've met have a strict routine that involves a variety of balancing points. One CEO I worked for prioritized his health during travel by finding small gyms that could accommodate his schedule before or after his meetings with employees. Another CEO hit the bike after a long day of meetings, spinning his stress away each night.

Others I've met have realized that their true balance comes from a deep peace in their spiritual and family lives, in that as long as those two are balanced, the rest can be worked out.

For me, this has been the foundation on which I have tried to live my life: God first, and the rest will be taken care of. Some days I've been successful, while other days, I've missed the mark.

This goes back to the encouragement my former boss, Conrad, gave me about selecting the five things that I would prioritize in my life. I haven't been perfect at managing all the pressures of work and life, but I've worked hard to keep God, my wife, and my kids as my top priorities. There are so many things that can consume us, but we should always be grounded in the five things that will drive our lives.

> **TIP:** Take time to reflect on the top five priorities in your life. Are these key priorities rock solid? Are the others in balance? Regularly reflect on the Rule of Five to ensure that you are prioritizing the most important things.

Your Team's Needs First

We can get so caught up in delivering on the operational expectations of the company, financial pressures, state or federal commitments, strategy, training, human resources, planning, and more. A leader's list is constantly filled with things to do, but it's important to keep our teams front and center.

We called this our "First Team," recognizing that my direct reports came first and that nothing came before our responsibility to one another. We took care of each other and leaned in whenever help was needed. It forced an ongoing question: Is your team truly coming first, or are you allowing their time and attention to dwindle? Are you listening to their needs? Are they a phone call, an open door, or a coffee away from you—or have they become so distant that you barely know how their families are doing, the latest sport their kids are playing, or the health of their elderly parents?

Your team comes first, and you must constantly place them at the top of your work relationships. The closer we get to our teams, the closer we get to the winning strategies we need to employ at the company. The closer we get, the better and more fruitful the work becomes. Don't allow anything to come between you and your team!

> **TIP:** Your time matters. The more responsibility you gain, the more you will encounter competition for your attention. Remember, your team comes first; give them the time they deserve.

Know the *Why* Behind the *What*

If the *why* is big enough, the *what* appears so small. The *why* matters so much that employees want to hear it all the time. It's where the good stuff lies. And when we don't share it with them, it is perceived that it is only to be known by those in the ivory towers of upper leadership, but nothing could be further from the truth.

The *why* matters to our employees, and they want to hear from us. Our employees want to know that we care enough to help them experience the *why* and join the mission behind it. Identifying it at every inflection point helps us deliver the message with passion, conviction, and a call to action.

> **TIP:** We are taught the *what*, but rarely taught the *why*. When the *why* is strong, people will follow.

Trouble Is the Privilege of a Leader

When times get tough, recognize that you've been given a privilege that few get. As a frontline employee, I rarely became aware of the troubles that were creeping throughout the organization. As I climbed the ladder, I became aware of problems monthly, then weekly, then daily, and sometimes multiple times per day.

This is a reminder that when trouble hits, stop to understand that you've been given a privilege that few get, embrace it, then face it. Don't wonder about why the problem came your way or whether you deserve it or not, the reality is that you signed up for it, and you need to weather these problems for the organization.

When you begin to understand this principle, problems become challenges you and your team want to conquer. These challenges often provide opportunities to grow individually and as a team.

I've never liked the phrase "Fake it until you make it." We need to be leaders who say, *"Face* it until you make it." In other words, embrace the problems that come your way.

> **TIP:** Learn to welcome the trouble. The more trouble that comes your way, the more you will train your mind and body that it will be okay. Doing this well helps us embrace trouble when it comes.

Give to Others What You Would Want from Others

How do you respond when an employee comes to you with news of trouble or failure? Do you respond graciously, recognizing their hard work, dedication, and effort? Or do you respond negatively to the failure?

Give those employees what you would want your own boss to bless you with in the future: empathy, understanding, support, and encouragement. The grace you give those employees will circle back to you in ways you would never imagine.

I've been blessed with leaders who wanted to do the right thing, many of whom are the best in their field, yet they fail from time to time. I have learned to grant them what I wish some of my early leaders would have granted me. You have wonderful leaders next to you; when they fail, walk with them through failure and up to success.

TIP: When your team encounters failure, remember that they've always been there for you. Give them the same grace you would want if you were in their shoes.

Feed the Good and Starve the Bad

What are you feeding today, and what are you starving? We all know that what we feed ends up flourishing, yet what we starve ends up dying.

Are you planning the day so you can actively feed what will grow you and your team with encouragement, support, engagement, development, and wisdom? Are you feeding them what they need to strengthen and accomplish their goals?

The most engaged employees are easy to spot. They encourage others, smile, bring joy to the work environment, and look for innovative ways to win as a team. Be on the lookout for what your employees are hungry for and feed that.

Are you starving when you show up? What habits are you killing day by day that create the opposite effect of flourishing?

We need to be cognizant of what we should be continuously working to eliminate from our speech and our actions. Starve micromanaging, procrastination, constant change, overworking employees, or anything else that can cripple the culture.

> **TIP:** Set the tone for how you will enter work each day. You have a tremendous opportunity to feed what matters and starve things that don't.

Discipline vs. Disappointment

Sometimes we know we need to act, but something holds us back. In those moments, we must have the discipline to do what's right or face disappointment through inaction. This could involve taking the necessary steps with an employee who does not fit the company's culture or making leadership decisions to ensure consistent results over time.

Part of leadership is having the discipline to follow through with tough decisions while also recognizing that if we don't, we will be disappointed. Disappointment can be avoided if we understand that discipline is important each day. Deal with the challenges that come your way quickly and effectively, and build teams that can do the same.

Ultimately, discipline is the foundation of safety, compliance, continuous improvement, and so much more. It is about establishing repeatable practices that allow us to deliver consistent results each and every day. Discipline gives leaders and teams the ability to act when it matters most—especially when it's uncomfortable—ensuring we do what's right, not what's easy. When discipline becomes a daily habit, it drives reliability, strengthens culture, and enables long-term success for individuals, teams, and the organization as a whole.

> **TIP:** Having discipline today minimizes the disappointments we will face tomorrow.

Build Teachers and Learners

Years ago, I started my all-hands meeting by telling my team, "This has been one of our best years yet for our team and the company as a whole. I know that because when I look around, I see teachers and learners."

I was seeing an engaged workforce that had put out one of the best years ever in safety, operational excellence, and quality, and they loved what they did. We had hit all our key metrics and evolved our planning processes, looking out ten to fifteen years. We had fewer vehicular accidents and no serious injuries or operational events. Employees wanted to teach others, and both new and seasoned team members wanted to learn.

We had built a passion and vision so strong that teams were building their legacy, becoming the teachers we needed, and discovering new ways of delivering on our business model. Are you building teachers who grow others? Do you have a culture that values learning?

> **TIP:** Recognize your teachers and learners and build them up within your organization.

FEEDBACK

Tell Me the Truth, Not What I Want to Hear

Your teams need to hear these words constantly. Telling the truth isn't optional; it is essential! Employees are often taught to say what senior leaders want to hear, but that should never be accepted.

Telling our employees to remove the filter of "tell me what I want to hear" puts them at ease that they will not be in jeopardy by telling the truth. I've gained some of the greatest insights, ultimately saving us from greater issues, from individuals who brought truth early.

> **TIP:** When truth comes your way, and it's not good news, don't react negatively. Remember that you wanted the truth.

Feedback is a Gift

I have spoken these words for years, but I didn't truly see feedback as a gift until employees started to say it back to me.

In Spanish, the word for feedback is *retroalimentación,* which can be translated as "looking back to nourish." I first heard the word when my parents and I were sitting at the Hilton in Panama City. That day, the front desk employee was completely disconnected from her job, focusing more on her phone than on her work. We kept calm, but when we sat down for a quick bite at the restaurant, we asked to see the manager to provide some feedback.

I will never forget the manager's face. He smiled and said, "Thank you so much. Our culture here is one of feedback, and this will help her grow." His goal was not to reprimand her but rather to help nourish her. His goal was to lift her up with the feedback we were providing, and it would be her choice to receive it or not.

Retroalimentación is to look back in time, realize what has occurred, and provide the nourishment needed for the future. I have looked at my employees in the same way, identifying ways that I can nourish them so they can grow.

Let's nourish others through feedback, and when someone comes to you with heartfelt retroalimentación, know that they are trying to nourish your soul, too.

> **TIP:** Receive and provide feedback.
> Remember, it nourishes the spirit!

Shine Light on Problems

It's been said that sunlight is the best disinfectant; we have to be ready to shine light on problems. Recognize the problems the company faces and embrace them head-on. Don't wait for them to grow, but work on the problems with tenacity and expediency. Shining the light on problems helps create a culture where others look for problems and drive resolution as well.

Turn finding problems into wins and thank your employees for bringing them to you.

Some of the best work I've seen my employees do has come from recognizing a problem and then tackling it as a team with full dedication and focus. They shed light where it was needed and responded when it became evident that change was necessary.

> **TIP:** Don't hide from an issue; shine a spotlight on it. Problems are opportunities to grow as a team.

Imagine the Risk

Some of the most significant process safety events in the world can be tied back to a lack of imagination. Create a culture each day where risks are discussed, allowing your teams to recognize the problems when they are on their own.

We must remember that complacency is waiting to creep up on us; we cannot be complacent with risk identification. Before you know it, that complacency will creep up on you and lead to failure. It's a leader's responsibility to discuss learnings from past events and share experiences to help prevent future occurrences. Creating these venues allows our teams to imagine that risks are out there and that we must do everything we can to prevent the next event from happening. Imagine the risk and teach your teams to do the same.

> **TIP:** The skill of imagination that we all learned in grade school opens our minds to find risk. Dream!

USING THE BAG OF TOOLS

My hope is that you take the time to look back at this chapter and pick out some of the areas that are most pertinent to the current stage of your leadership journey. Read the sections and place yourself in your situation at work. Pick a few of these tools that you can begin to apply with your teams today.

I also encourage you to start building your own repertoire of stories, anecdotes, sayings, and reminders to help you. The tools in this chapter have been invaluable to me at various stages of my own journey. Each year, I have learned a little more about a certain topic, experienced another lesson with my team, and jotted it down for when the next challenge comes my way.

Make these tools your own and add yours to this list. Share this bag of tools with your team as you continue to grow together.

GET TO WORK

1. Which tool from this chapter do you depend on most,

and how can you use it with greater intention in your daily leadership?

2. Which tool do you most often neglect, and what is one small action you can take this week to strengthen it?

3. How will you build a consistent daily rhythm of reflecting, learning, and connecting with others that keeps all your leadership tools sharp over time?

CONCLUSION

"*A good person leaves an inheritance
for their children's children...*"
Proverbs 13:22 NIV

Legacy is all around us. The companies that we work in, the families and communities we are part of, and the cities we live in were built by pioneers who have gone before us. Our best leadership books, podcasts, and teachings come from those who have led their own legacy. For previous generations, we are a fulfillment of their legacy. We can carry on their positive characteristics while paving our own path.

Every day, we have a choice of how we want to lead. Are we going to keep our eyes on our legacy and build a culture and people who will outlast us? Or will we get stuck in a myopic rut?

The foundation for any leader is their character. The truth is that we cannot lead a legacy for our companies, families, and communities if we are leading out of dysfunction. Self-reflection and self-improvement are necessary for leaders at all levels. When we understand who we are and invest in ourselves, we can then pour into others. When we are able to set our egos aside, we can celebrate the people around us.

Collaboration becomes easier when we are secure in who we are.

From that place of internal health, we can then turn to those around us and those we have the privilege of leading. We can focus on the most important part of any company:

the people.

As leaders, it's our privilege to serve the people on our teams and in our companies. We lead a legacy in how we focus on our people by investing in them, celebrating them, challenging them, and championing them. When we create a people-centric culture, we are creating something that will long outlast us. A positive legacy comes from caring for our people, keeping them safe, and helping them understand the legacy they will leave behind.

I've spent my life trying to understand how I can serve people better and lead a legacy that stands the test of time. This question has driven me and even kept me awake at night: How does legacy endure? How does it become more than a name, title, or fleeting moment of recognition?

For me, the answer lies in the people, the ones you serve, the ones you nurture, and most importantly, the ones who will carry your legacy forward. In my case, that's my four boys: William, Henry, Oliver, and Winston. From the moment they were born, they became part of my story.

Every decision I've made in my career, and every move we've made as a family, has been with them in mind. I wanted them to see and understand that legacy isn't just about what you leave behind; it's about what you build, step by step, day by day, and how it impacts the lives of others.

When I think of legacy, I think of purpose and the ways we shape the world around us. My wife, Hili, and I have always tried to involve our boys in the decisions we've made. When we moved from Arizona to California, for example, William and Henry were still young, but we made sure they understood the purpose behind our move. We told them that we were going to California because PG&E needed help in recovering. We didn't just tell them about the tragedy; we made sure they understood that we were part of something much bigger than ourselves. We were going to help make sure something like that wouldn't happen again. That simple truth, that our work and lives were about making things safer for others, was the foundation of everything that followed.

Later, as we drove through what remained of San Bruno, passing the cleared land where once homes stood, I saw something shift in my family. The boys weren't old enough to understand every detail, but as we moved through the remnants of what had once been a vibrant community, I could see them beginning to grasp the weight of the choices we had made. In that moment, they started to sense that our decisions carried purpose tied to the communities we served. Over the years, we have continued to talk about my work as a family: why we moved, why those moves mattered, and why getting safety right is so important. Through those conversations, they've come to understand that our legacy was never just about a job or a paycheck. It was about people. It was about lives. And most of all, it was about safety.

That belief in safety has been at the core of every move, every career shift, and every choice we've made as a family. When we moved to Ohio in 2019 to support NiSource after the Merrimack Valley Incident, I had a similar conversation with the boys. By this time, three out of our four boys were old enough to understand the significance of the work. As a father of four boys, this story was deeply personal to me. It reminded me of my sons—and of the unimaginable pain and suffering a family endures after such a tragic loss. It also helped them better understand the sacrifices Hilary and I had made, uprooting our family multiple times as I supported organizations in the aftermath of tragedy. Before our move, I told them about Leonel Rondon, the young man who lost his life in the incident. I explained that my role in the recovery effort was to help ensure no other family would have to experience the loss of someone they love—that we were stepping into something bigger than ourselves, work that mattered, work meant to prevent such tragedies from ever happening again.

As I watched my boys take in the weight of those words, I knew that our purpose was becoming clear to them. The idea of legacy was no longer abstract. It wasn't just about words or stories; it was about action. It was about shaping the future in ways that would make our communities a better place for everyone.

For Hili and me, this isn't about career progression or industry recognition. It's about showing our boys that they, too, can lead a legacy that will stand the test of time. It's about giving them the tools and the understanding to lead with integrity, compassion, and a relentless drive to make the world safer for the generations to come.

That's the essence of what we're doing. It's not just about a career. It's about planting the seeds of a future that is defined not by the mistakes of the past, but by the lessons learned. We want our boys to understand that their legacy will not be defined by the jobs they choose or the wealth they accumulate; it will be defined by the people they serve and the values they uphold. Legacy is built, slowly but surely, with every act of service, every decision made with care, and every effort to ensure that the next generation is better protected than the last.

You don't need a shocking experience to take action; I believe everyone should wake up each day and ask, "What can I do to put people first, care for them, and honor what God has given me by prioritizing their well-being and their growth?"

No one said it better than the biblical figure, King Solomon, who ruled Israel. Near the end of his life, he wrote,

> I said to myself, "Come on, let's try pleasure. Let's look for the 'good things' in life." But I found that this, too,

was meaningless. … I also tried to find meaning by building huge homes for myself and by planting beautiful vineyards. I made gardens and parks, filling them with all kinds of fruit trees. … I also owned large herds and flocks, more than any of the kings who had lived in Jerusalem before me. I collected great sums of silver and gold, the treasure of many kings and provinces. … I had everything a man could desire!

So, I became greater than all who had lived in Jerusalem before me, and my wisdom never failed me. Anything I wanted, I would take. I denied myself no pleasure. I even found great pleasure in hard work, a reward for all my labors. But as I looked at everything I had worked so hard to accomplish, it was all so meaningless—like chasing the wind. There was nothing really worthwhile anywhere. Ecclesiastes 2:1, 4-5, 7b-8a, 8b-11 (NLT)

What an amazing look back at life by a man who tried it all. Well said, King Solomon! What really matters most isn't our accomplishments or possessions but the legacy that we leave behind. For King Solomon, his legacy came from the work he did for the people of Israel, building the first temple for the Israelites and utilizing wisdom throughout his reign. His name and legacy have been imprinted in history, and we can all gain valuable wisdom from his life's journey.

Now that you've learned more about my life and legacy, I invite you to reflect on the meaning of legacy. Take some time to answer these questions:

- What will your legacy be?
- How will you serve others?
- How will your actions shape the world for those who come after you?

Legacy is not just something you leave behind; it's something you create. It's something that grows, like the roots of a great tree, reaching down into the soil and anchoring you to the future. For me, that legacy is clear: it's about people and safety, most importantly, creating a world where my boys and the generations that follow can thrive.

This is how a legacy stands the test of time. It is built not on monuments or accolades, but on the lives you touch, the people you serve, and the safety and love you instill in the hearts of those who will carry it forward.

As I reflect on the journey we've walked together through these pages, one thing becomes abundantly clear for me: God has been so good and so faithful. His presence has guided me through every challenge, every triumph, and every moment of uncertainty. He has shown me time and again that when we commit to His purpose, placing people at the heart of everything we do, He will lead us to a legacy that transcends our own efforts and impacts the world around us.

Now, as you stand on the other side of this book, I urge you not to wait too long to search for your own legacy. Time moves quickly. It's easy to get caught up in the rush of everyday life, but before you know it, the years will slip away. Don't wait until it's too late. Start now. Start today. Begin seeking a purpose bigger than yourself. Pursue a purpose that isn't driven by accolades, power, or success, but one that centers on people. A purpose that places the needs, growth, and well-being of others at the heart of your work and your life. This is the legacy that will endure.

I encourage you to take one principle you've learned from this book and begin to implement it in your life. Maybe it's taking the time to invest in your own character. Perhaps it's focusing on working with your team to cast a powerful, inspiring vision. Or maybe you're in the midst of a challenge and need to walk through the four phases of rebuilding. Maybe you've just stepped into a new role, and you need to put people first and prioritize their growth. Whatever your situation may be, pick one principle, focus on it, and gain competence in it. Once you feel grounded in that area, move to the next. Leadership is a lifelong journey, and each step forward is part of building the legacy you are meant to lead and leave.

I also encourage you to revisit Chapter 10 (The Bag of Tools) whenever you need inspiration or encouragement. The tools are not just theoretical; they're practical, actionable steps that can help you navigate any situation. Practice those tools. Refine them. Build your own set of tools that you can rely on when the going gets tough.

But here's the most important part: Don't let the lessons you've learned or the tools you've gained end with you. A key part of leading a legacy is sharing what you know with others. You've learned from the wisdom of respected leaders throughout this book; now it's your turn to pass that knowledge forward. Whether it's to your team, your family, or your community, invest in others. Teach them the principles that have helped you, and show them the tools that have shaped your journey.

What tools can you share with your team to help them start building their own legacy? What principles can you teach them to help them grow as leaders? Don't let your knowledge stay with you. Empower others to walk the same path of growth, purpose, and legacy.

Most of all, keep investing in the people around you. People are the most important part of any company, any team, any family. Your ability to develop and invest in them will be the true measure of your legacy. Continue to share, encourage, and build up the people you lead.

I want to applaud you for taking the time to invest in yourself and your leadership. This journey of leading a legacy is not an easy one, but it is so worth it. It is a beautiful, fulfilling process that will not only shape your future but will also have a profound impact on those around you. Your future is bright.

Keep pressing forward. Lead with purpose and vision, keeping people at the center of everything you do. The impact you make will ripple far beyond what you can see.

Your team, your company, and your community will thank you for it. And one day, when you look back, you'll be proud of the legacy you've created.

Today is the only day you are guaranteed to lead your legacy.

Not tomorrow. Not "someday." Today.

And as Micah 6:8 reminds us, God has already shown us what is good: to do justly, to love mercy, and to walk humbly with our God. This is not abstract theology; it is a blueprint for leadership.

This is the kind of leadership that leaves a legacy worth remembering, one where people and safety are at the center of every plan, every strategy, and every decision.

My challenge to you is simple and urgent: start your legacy today.

- Do the just thing, even when it costs you, especially when no one is watching.
- Choose mercy when it would be easier to turn away; slow down, listen, see the whole person, and respond in a way that protects both their dignity and their future.
- Walk humbly, listening, learning, and never becoming casual about risk, because lives, families, and communities depend on the choices you make.

If you will lead like that, seeing danger and taking refuge, doing justice, loving mercy, and walking humbly, your legacy will not be a final chapter you write at the end of your career.

It will be written day by day, decision by decision,

in the lives you protected,

in the people you developed,

and in the communities you faithfully served.

As you step forward from these pages and into the reality of your own leadership, remind yourself that the work is both urgent and deeply personal. Ask the questions that matter: *What tools, skills, mindsets, and habits am I relying on, and are they still serving me in the challenges of today? What tools am I missing that I must develop to lead with greater clarity and conviction? How deliberately am I sharpening those tools through reflection, feedback, mentorship, and continuous learning?*

The answers to these questions become more than self-assessments; they become the foundation of the legacy you are building. Because legacy is not a distant finish line. As Richard Ferry reminds us, it begins now, in the present, in the ordinary moments that reveal who we are long before they define what we leave behind. Legacy is shaped in the way we treat people, in the sincerity of our gratitude, in the courage of our decisions, and in the quiet consistency of showing up with heart. It compounds over time, collecting in the stories others tell about how we made them feel, how we helped them grow, and how we led when it mattered. This is the real work. This is the invitation. And it is yours to answer.

Your journey is just beginning. Do not wait. Start building your legacy now.

"Legacy begins here, in the present, in the day-to-day that reveals not just what we do, but also who we truly are."

"Above all else, guard your heart, for
everything you do flows from it."
Proverbs 4:23 NIV

THANK YOU FOR READING MY BOOK!

Thanks for buying and reading my book. I would like to connect!

Scan the QR code:

I appreciate your interest in my book and value your feedback, as it helps me improve future versions. I would appreciate it if you could leave your invaluable review on Amazon.com with your feedback. Thank you!

www.ingramcontent.com/pod-product-compliance
Lightning Source LLC
Chambersburg PA
CBHW031925190326
41519CB00007B/421